The

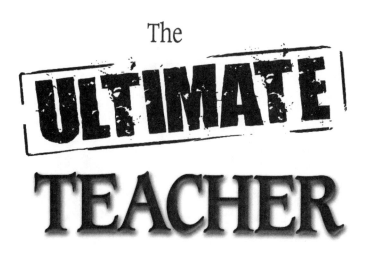

ULTIMATE TEACHER

The Best Experts' Advice for a Noble Profession with Photos and Stories

Todd Whitaker
author of *What Great Teachers Do
Differently: 14 Things That Matter Most*

Health Communications, Inc.
HCI Books, the Life Issues Publisher
Deerfield Beach, Florida

www.hcibooks.com
www.ultimatehcibooks.com

We would like to acknowledge the writers who granted us permission to use their material. Copyright credits for literary works are listed alphabetically by authors' last names. Contact information as supplied by the writers can be found in the back matter of this book.

The Odyssey. © Christa B. Allan.

A Sea of White. © Donna Amato.

Stop Poist. © Chris Bancells.

(Copyright Credits continued on page 277)

Library of Congress Cataloging-in-Publication Data
is available through the Library of Congress.

© 2009 Health Communications, Inc.

ISBN-13: 978-0-7573-0797-3
ISBN-10: 0-7573-0797-3

Publisher: Health Communications, Inc.
3201 S.W. 15th Street
Deerfield Beach, FL 33442-8190

Cover Design: Justin Rotkowitz
Photo: © Getty Images
Photo Editor: Justin Rotkowitz
Interior Design: Lawna Patterson Oldfield
Interior Formatting: Dawn Von Strolley Grove

*For my mother, Avis, whose calmness and
sense of humor permeates my life;*

my wife Beth, who makes me a better person each day;

*and my three children, Katherine, Madeline, and Harrison,
who make my life complete.*

Thank you for all you have taught me.

Is something "Ultimately" important to you? Then we want to know about it. . . .

We hope you enjoyed *The Ultimate Teacher*. We are planning many more books in the Ultimate series, each filled with entertaining stories, must-know facts, and captivating photos. We're always looking for talented writers to share slice-of-life true stories, creative photographers to capture images that a story can't tell, as well as top experts to offer their unique insights on a given topic.

For more information on submission guidelines, or to suggest a topic for an upcoming book, please visit the Ultimate website at **www.ultimatehcibooks.com**, or write to: Submission Guidelines, Ultimate Series, HCI Books, 3201 SW 15th St., Deerfield Beach, FL 33442.

For more information about other books by Health Communications, Inc., please visit **www.hcibooks.com**.

Contents

v

New Teachers

Teaching by Example

A Teacher's Caring Heart

Must-Know Info

Introduction

The Ultimate Teacher: every educator aspires to this pinnacle of success. Teaching is a profession that makes a difference every single day—on both sides of the desk. Virtually all of us can remember the kindness, caring, and humor of the special people who taught us when we were their students. Many of them shaped our minds and touched our hearts. Their impact was immeasurable and on-going.

No matter how old you were or what grade you were in when you connected with that special teacher, you know that the unique gifts a great teacher shares stay with you forever.

Do you recall how you felt when your favorite teacher read a thought-provoking story to your class? Do you remember the teacher who taught you how to multiply when you were so frustrated you wanted to give up, or the teacher who knew when you needed encouragement, or the one who gave you breathing room when you needed just that? The "special something" these ultimate teachers possess continues to remind all of us in this profession why we chose to be educators ourselves.

Unfortunately, many students come from homes where there

may not be a stable environment or a consistent and positive role model. Many times, teachers are these students' last and best hope. It is essential that each child walk into a classroom—every day—to the teacher who inspires by example. Education's goal is to cultivate society, not to reflect it. We have to teach and model new and better ways each day in our classrooms.

A teacher's influence can last a lifetime. We all chose a career in education for different reasons, but we share the common desire to make a difference—yet some days we lose touch with that initial passion. Sometimes, when we have a challenging day or face a troubling class, we may forget the difference we can make for each and every student. On those days, you'll find the stories in this book to be a treasure trove of inspiration and innovation. You'll be motivated to try other teachers' novel techniques as you read about their challenges, their memorable students, and the times they knew they made an impact. You'll walk into the classrooms of some of the most gifted and caring educators in the world, and share their memories of humorous happenings and poignant moments. You'll delight in the recollections of some of those students themselves, and you'll learn from the mentoring advice of some special experts whose best teaching tips will resonate with new and experienced educators alike.

A very wise person once told me, "Those who can, teach. Those who can't go into a much less significant line of work." Good reading and thanks for making a difference.

Teachers
Who Inspire

The Soul of a Poet Award

By Donna Watson

Every year I bestow a unique award. I never plan to give it; I never know which student will earn it. I call it the Soul of a Poet Award. This award's inception began almost two decades ago, during student teaching.

As a student teacher, I found it difficult to reach struggling students, especially in the critical subject areas of reading and writing. Understandably, they feared taking risks or making mistakes in front of their more capable, and sometimes quick to taunt, classmates. Jake was one of my first challenging students. An underachiever who had been plunked inappropriately into a "Gifted and Talented" fourth-grade class, Jake struggled daily to keep up with his precocious classmates. In a room overflowing with overanxious hand-raisers, Jake remained sullen and silent, until the day we picked up our pencils to pen a bit of poetry.

As I wrote the topic on the board, I remember thinking that this assignment might be a tough sell. "Today we will write a single sentence using a metaphor to describe love."

Not surprisingly, half of the class responded with a collective groan. They were, after all, nine- and ten-year-olds. Their ears perked up a bit upon learning that their responses and accompanying artwork would be submitted for possible publication in the local newspaper for Valentine's Day.

As I wandered around the room monitoring their work and commenting with a perfunctory "Good job!" or "Nice work!" I happened to glance down at Jake's paper.

"Love is peanut butter and jelly and all that makes me feel sticky and gooey inside."

He cautiously glanced up at me. The words, penned in crayon, sprang out of a giant red heart. I stifled my first reaction. I had specifically stated that the words must be written in pencil. Jake, once again, neglected to follow directions. But I resisted the urge to admonish him for writing in crayon, especially on an assignment headed for the newspaper.

We shared a tentative smile. I had no idea that my next response would resound for years to come: "Why Jake, I think you have the soul of a poet!"

Apparently the newspaper editors agreed, for when I opened the Valentine's Day issue, Jake's declaration of love burst right off the front page of the "Features" section.

I finished student teaching not long afterward to begin my solo teaching journey, packing away more than just books and papers as I left.

I have found that through poetry writing and personal essays, students face fears, examine prejudices, and overcome personal obstacles. Annually, my students write poems about Martin Luther King, Jr., Ruby Bridges, Johnny Appleseed, favorite book characters, their families, and themselves. Children respond with gut-wrenching honesty and heartfelt integrity through writing. Even the shiest students scamper to the circle to share their individual thoughts.

Year after year, my Soul of a Poet Award is bestowed upon a most unlikely candidate. This past September, Mark rocketed into my second-grade classroom. Angry, defiant, torn from his father's home, his friends, and the only school he had ever attended, Mark opposed any form of structure. My numerous and previously effective behavior-management tricks folded as he systematically played his hand. Parent phone calls, trips to the principal's office, recess detention—nothing fazed Mark.

Bright but underachieving, Mark challenged authority at every turn. In my two decades of teaching, he held the dubious distinction as my most frustrating student. Slowly, very slowly, we established a tenuous bond. As the year progressed, Mark continued to press every nerve while simultaneously stealing my heart. Daily, he filled me with frustration and pride.

Writing seemed to allow Mark to release some of his anger and frustration in a healthier outlet. Over time, I noticed a gradual, positive shift in his behavior. When asked to write what was bothering him, Mark first just scratched the surface, but as the year went on, he placed his problems on paper rather than trying to solve them with inappropriate words or physical contact. Although I have witnessed this kind of constructive conversion with other difficult students, Mark's transformation encouraged and amazed me.

The bio-poem the students publish for open house at the end of the year remains my favorite. The format allows the students to expose their innermost thoughts and feelings. Every year I'm awestruck by the maturity some second-graders possess and project in their final poem about themselves. As Mark and the other students wrote, they asked me to spell words for their student dictionary. Mark asked for several words, each one more thought-provoking than the last. I told him I was anxious to hear his poem, knowing he had selected several "hundred-dollar" adjectives.

We gathered in our circle to share our prized poems. Mark waved his poem in my face like a checkered flag at a NASCAR race. It seemed to torture him to wait his turn, but once he began to read, I understood his sense of urgency to share.

Mark's masterpiece was worth the wait:

Mark

By Mark, age 8

I touch God's heavenly hands.

I dream of thousands of books scattered everywhere.

I want my father and mother to be with me always.

I am Mark.

I hear the sun up in the sky.

I wonder if my dad will be with me always.

I live on planet Earth.

I am Mark, the pleasant young man I was born to be.

I see the moon light the sky.

I like when we get to go to school.

I fear my Nana's cat.

I am Mark, the generous young man I was created to be.

I pretend to be in the army.

I cry when somebody goes away.

I love my whole family.

I am Mark, the generous, adventurous American Boy I was
    created to be.

Mark's chestnut brown eyes sparkled as he savored my
response: "Mark, you have the soul of a poet!"

A Gym-Dandy Coach

By Woody Woodburn

I t was like being awakened by the telephone at three in the morning. Like having a police officer knock on your door at dinnertime. You instinctively know it's not good news.

My heart raced double-time as I read the writing on the wall during a visit to my old middle school: MCFADDEN GYM.

Ring . . . ring . . . ring . . . Knock-knock-knock.

Gymnasiums and football stadiums are very much like statues. Statues are chiseled and sculpted to honor dead war heroes; gyms are usually christened after dead sport champions.

I hoped against hope that McFadden Gym was the rare exception to the rule, for I knew who the gym was named after: Harold R. McFadden. Coach McFadden. My favorite gym teacher—in fact, my favorite teacher of all time.

For the most part, the names of the teachers I had when I roamed Balboa Junior High in Ventura, California, in the early 1970s are lost in the cobwebs of my mind. Oh, sure, I remember my shop teacher, Mr. Howell. And Mrs. Stewart, who I had for English, seemingly every semester. And Mr. Nelson, my good friend Mike's dad, who I had for math once.

But Coach McFadden was special. He was a diamond among rhinestones. A star among moons. He was an MVP if the teaching profession gave out such an award. When I think of Balboa, I think of Coach McFadden.

And when I think of Coach McFadden, I instantly think of athletic shoes. Fresh-out-of-the-shoebox new sneakers.

You see, I had the great fortune of having Coach McFadden for PE five of my six semesters at Balboa. I saw him every day, and every day, sunshine or rain, he had on a new pair of athletic shoes. Or so it seemed.

Actually, he only broke out a fresh pair of footgear three or four times a year. Christmas presents and birthday presents, he once told me. But he had more than a dozen old pairs of athletic shoes that *looked* brand-spankin' new. Maybe twenty pairs. His secret, he gladly shared, was to clean them after every wearing—just like my grandpa used to do with his wingtip dress shoes. But instead of shoe polish and a soft cloth, Coach McFadden found that an old, soft toothbrush and some liquid dishwashing soap did the trick nicely.

So it just appeared as though Coach McFadden wore new shoes every day: red suede Converse low-top All-Stars on Monday, white Tigers (now called Asics) running shoes on Tuesday, blue Chuck Taylor Converse high-tops on Wednesday, Adidas Superstars with red stripes on Thursday, Adidas with blue stripes on Friday, and white and blue Nikes the next Monday.

To be sure, Coach McFadden was more than just a pretty pair of size 9½ feet. More than a male Imelda Marcos of the locker room. He was a superstar gym teacher. Even back then, three decades ago, he was coaching kids to say no to drugs, imploring us to hit the books, not just the basketball backboards and pitches in the strike zone.

Most of all, he encouraged us to *try*.

The stereotypical gym coach is a dour drillmaster Simon Legree with a clipboard and whistle. Coach McFadden was cut from a different sweatshirt cloth. He never raised his voice, never frowned, and was never at a loss for a few warm words. He whipped his students into shape with kindness and encouragement. He made the medicine taste like a spoonful of sugar.

Specifically, I vividly recall that he used to add one more push-up every week during our warm-up calisthenics, and by the end of the semester even the out-of-shape couch potatoes were down and doing twenty.

He swayed selfish gunners to play selfless team-style basketball. Some kids he turned on to wrestling, some on to track. He tried to turn every kid into some kind of athlete. If you couldn't be a Bullet Bob sprinter, he urged, be a Distance Demon. *Try*. Be the best you can be.

A yardstick for any junior high gym instructor is the number of students who don't dress out for class. Coach McFadden's classes, I'm certain, set the standard for the lowest number of "nondressers" in PE history.

Now, I must admit that Coach McFadden wasn't perfect. He never did get me to do a respectable handstand, for instance.

But my sneakers always looked newer, thanks to him. They still do.

Indeed, for the last thirty-something years, every time I've meticulously laced up a new pair of athletic shoes—or laced on ones that I've scrubbed with a soft, old toothbrush and dish-washing soap—I've thought of Coach McFadden. Even seeing new sneakers on someone else or walking by a Footlocker store brings him to my mind.

Ring . . . ring . . . ring . . . Knock-knock-knock.

My worst fears were indeed true. Returning to my middle school after having moved away for a long time, I saw his name on the gym and did some research. I found out that Coach McFadden died after battling cancer in 1984, exactly ten years after my last PE class with him and long before he had a chance to lose the hop on his fastball or the shrill in his whistle. He was far too young at age fifty-four. Finding out all these years later didn't ease the pain one bit.

I'm glad my old junior high rechristened its gym in honor of Harold R. McFadden. It's even more heartening to know that it became "Mac's Gym"—as it is most often called—a year *before* Coach McFadden succumbed.

I'm glad Coach Mac got to see MCFADDEN GYM, for as Nixon Waterman once wrote, "A rose to the living is more / Than sumptuous wreaths to the dead."

Excuse me now, please. I have to go clean my Nike Air Max 360s before the teardrops leave a stain.

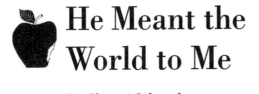

He Meant the World to Me

By Charmi Schroeder

Each week, we'd run to the bulletin board of Mr. Everson's seventh-grade geography classroom. We couldn't wait to see that week's amazing pictures. There was always one place that everyone in the class recognized so that we'd all get at least one extra-credit point. But the other pictures often required research.

In the evenings, my parents would listen to my descriptions and help me decipher where the magical pictures might be.

"It was so cool! The tops looked like a Dairy Queen ice-cream cone!"

Mom and Dad smiled, and we were off to the library to find a book on Russia. They let me look through it until I found a picture of the building matching the one on the board. Then we checked out the book, and I read all about it. I insisted that Mom and Dad add Moscow to our vacation list for the summer.

On to the next picture.

"They have the neatest statue you've ever seen! All these people stuck together. It's just wild!" Mr. E. only posted a picture of one sculpture at Vigeland Sculpture Park in Oslo, Norway, but I wanted to see all 212. I made my parents promise that when we went, we'd spend the whole day there.

And the next picture.

"It looks like sailboats on the harbor. It's just *beautiful!*" I spent the week reading about Australia. And my parents tried to figure out when and how they'd take their only daughter—the persistent one with the growing wanderlust—to Sydney.

I reveled in the moments when I walked up to the board and realized that there were pictures of places we'd visited. The Grand Canyon. The Space Needle. The St. Louis Arch. Mount Rushmore. Volcanoes National Park. I was so proud when I could tell Mr. E. about the places firsthand. I was even prouder when I could sit down at dinner and tell my parents that Mr. E. had posted pictures of places they'd already taken me to.

By the end of the school year, I'd accumulated close to one hundred extra-credit points. I'd read dozens of books about places that I never knew existed. I also had a notebook full of places to see as soon as I could—from Sydney to San Francisco, Oslo to the Outer Banks. I'd scoped them out in detail. I'd written down the highlights to explore, foods to eat, and things to buy in each place. I'd checked out almost every *Fodor's* and *Frommer's* travel guide in the library at one point during the 1976–77 school year—some of them twice. There were more travel brochures in my bedroom than at the travel agency. We were going to be very busy!

I loved learning about all these new places, and every week was a new adventure. I hated for the year to end, although I'm sure my parents were more than a little relieved!

I'm very fortunate to have parents who have always enjoyed traveling. We weren't rich—Dad worked in the factory in town and Mom worked in a grocery store—but I didn't know it. I just knew that every summer the factory shut down for a few weeks, and we loaded up the station wagon and went on great vacations. Now I had a huge list of new places for us to explore.

Mom and Dad made a plan. First, we'd see all fifty states, Canada, Mexico, and the Caribbean. Then we'd move on to Europe, the South Pacific, and Australia. We visited Australia two years after I graduated from college. We had dinner and saw a show at the Sydney Opera House—and it was just as beautiful as Mr. E.'s picture.

I remember looking over the edge of Niagara Falls totally in awe of the power and grace of the water rushing at my feet and remembering the photo tacked on Mr. E.'s classroom wall of where I now stood. One afternoon in Paris, I sat in a café in Montmartre looking at the Sacré-Coeur Basilica glistening in the sun. It was a beautiful sight—every bit as magnificent as I'd imagined a half-dozen years earlier.

We haven't visited every place that Mr. E. posted on that board. But we've certainly made a large dent in the list. And even though it's thirty years later, we're still planning family vacations to some of those places we researched together so many years ago.

A few years ago, I wrote Mr. E. a letter to thank him for giving a young girl a world of dreams. We've been corresponding and sharing postcards of our current travels ever since.

So again, thank you, Mr. Everson. You were a great teacher then, and you are a great friend now. You've quite literally meant the world to me.

The Unwise Monkey

By Joyce Stark

My aunt, Jessie Davidson, was a schoolteacher until she was well into her sixties. She must have been in her eighties when I was doing some dusting for her and picked up the brass "three wise monkeys" ornament that always had a place of pride on her dresser.

"I have many things I've received from pupils in my long career, and I cherish every single one of them," she told me. "I have many letters of thanks and little gifts from those I maybe took a little more trouble with. Quite a number are from those I used to lean the hardest on, showing that, despite my criticisms, they'd really turn out well! This gift means more to me than any other," she said, picking up the three wise monkeys. "I used a set of these in my lessons to try to teach the children the importance of tolerance and discretion. Hear no evil, see no evil, and speak no evil—I used to drum these words into them day after day. That's when I crossed swords with little Hamish McDonald!

"My word was law in those days," she continued. "Not

many children argued back at me, except Hamish, of course! He was a clever enough student, but he tended to get into arguments and fights more than the rest of them.

"When I was drumming the three wise monkeys into them one day, I saw him looking out the window. I walked up to him and said, 'This lesson applies more to you than to anyone here. Why aren't you paying attention?'

"Calm as day he looked at me and said, 'It's cowardly, that's why. Pretending you can't see, pretending you don't hear, and not speaking up when you should. I don't want to be that kind of person!'

"Just before he finished the term that year, Hamish's mother died of cancer. She was only in her thirties and the whole family was devastated. I told Hamish to stay after class when he returned to school after a few days off. I sat him down and said that despite our differences, I felt very sad for him. I told him that if he ever felt he needed someone he could talk to, he could always come to me. He cried a little that day; he was so vulnerable, and I held him.

"Eventually he stood up and looked at me almost sheepishly. 'This doesn't mean I agree with what you tell us,' he said defensively.

"I smiled at him. 'I would be disappointed if it did. I'm going to tell you something, Hamish, that might help you a little on your road through life. I want you to get your Bible and read again the story of the prodigal son. You see, the prodigal son didn't always follow the same lines as those around him, and sometimes that led him into a lot of trouble. But not once in all of the times he wandered from the path did Jesus love him any less. In fact, sometimes, because his path was more difficult and lonelier, Jesus loved him more.'

"I lost touch with Hamish within a few months; his father moved the family to England to be nearer his sister.

"One day a few years ago, a couple called here to see me. The young woman explained that she was the daughter of Hamish McDonald. She told me that her father had gone on to attend the university and qualified as a doctor. He had a number of posts but used to get extremely frustrated at all the anomalies of our medical system here in Scotland, so he ended up going to Africa, involved in some kind of medical aid project. He found so much to do there that he came back only rarely. That's where he met his wife, who was also involved in the same kind of work. Eventually he and his wife split up and his daughter and her brother came back with their mother to live in Scotland.

"The daughter explained that she always kept in contact with her dad, and the bond between them remained strong. He got involved in fights for better water, better food, and new hospitals, and often had tremendous arguments with those in authority. She used to visit him, and one thing he always took with him was a set of three brass monkeys. She remembered seeing the ornament, even when he was living in a makeshift tent, and asked him about it.

"He explained that a teacher called Mrs. Davidson had

given it to him and told him a story that he remembered every time he looked at it. Whenever things seemed impossible, and it felt as if everyone was against him, he remembered that conversation and kept going.

"Hamish's daughter told me that he achieved great things, and the local people just adored him. Ultimately, he picked up a virus and died there. Among his things, she found his precious three wise monkeys. She remembered his request: 'When something finally happens to me, I want you to take this and try to find Mrs. Davidson. She may well be dead, but she was young when she was my teacher, so maybe not. Give it to her and tell her how much she inspired me. Tell her it's from her Unwise Monkey.'"

My aunt wiped a tear off her cheek as she spoke. "I'm so proud of him. He spent most of his life fighting on other people's behalf. I think God always meant for him to be my Unwise Monkey, don't you?"

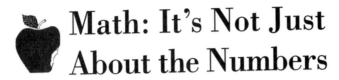

Math: It's Not Just About the Numbers

By Carrie Pepper

As I look at all of the smooth rocks and sparkling gemstones I've collected over the years, I think back to my first geology class in junior college. One of the prerequisites for that class was Algebra 1. Sure, I'd taken algebra back in high school. In fact, I'd taken the course twice. Each time, my report card reflected my struggles with a D—a stigma of failure alongside my As and Bs in other subjects. It just didn't sink in. All of those x's and y's made absolutely no sense to me. Being shy didn't help either. When it came time to raise my hand, I couldn't. "Do you understand?" the teacher would ask. No, I didn't understand. Yet I remained silent, terrified of revealing this to anyone else. Surely, they understood the problem. I sat staring at all the numbers and letters up there on the chalkboard, my heart racing with confusion, until I was nauseous. I didn't dare raise my hand.

My senior year was a repeat: same class, same teacher, same results. He seemed to cater to the boys. They understood math; they were to be architects and engineers. What would a girl do with algebra? She belonged next door in home economics class, sewing and cooking. We moved into more complex problems and I fell further and further behind.

Ten years later, I decided to follow my dream of becoming a geologist. I loved rocks and gems and the idea of going on field trips to study them. There it was again, right there on the requirements list: Algebra 1. Fear consumed me. I'd never get through it. At least I thought so, until I met Mr. Evans. The first time I walked by his office window and saw that big wooden paddle the size of an oar, I knew he was different. He'd always kid around that he used it on the more difficult students. He never paddled me, but I was definitely a challenge. Or should I say math was the challenge for me?

I had to pass the course. Without it, I couldn't move into higher mathematics. I was older now, but still painfully shy. But I had learned something: if I didn't raise my hand, if I just sat there quietly, I'd get passed along once again and no one would care.

Sitting in Mr. Evans's classroom, it all seemed the same. The problem was on the board in white chalk, as confusing as ever. Then I heard the voice and the question that always instilled such fear in the past: "Carrie, do you understand?" The words hung in the air; time slowed. All the years and classes and problems came flooding back. I would remain silent. I couldn't let anyone know I was completely and utterly lost. Then, almost involuntarily, my hand began to slowly ascend toward the ceiling, like a white flag in surrender, in full view of everyone. I felt eyes upon me, their stares drilling into me. *What's wrong with her? She doesn't understand?* I'd done it. I'd admitted my weakness, my confusion. Mr. Evans patiently took up the chalk and went through the problem again. Then he asked me a second time, "Do you understand now?" I wanted so badly to nod *yes*, to proudly let him know I had grasped the concept. But I didn't. *No*, I shook my head. *No. I'm a total failure. I don't understand. I cannot do this math. I am a girl, not a geologist.* He explained the problem a third time, and still I shook my head. Failure. Doom. Then he called me to his desk. "Come to my office at lunchtime," was all he said. And I did.

I visited him at lunchtime nearly every day after that. He sat and graded papers while I worked on problems at his side. He shared his cookies. There was no pressure or judgment. It was almost as if my father and I were working together, having a snack. Little by little, things began to click. I could do this math. I could understand. Maybe there was a chance for me.

And then, time came for the final exam. Panic set in. Tests were a whole different arena of fear. I'd always frozen during timed testing. I couldn't focus on the problems at hand, but only on the clock on the wall and the other students. I'd sit still, my eyes darting around the room, looking first at yellow pencils moving across test booklets, then at the huge hands on the clock face, my heart racing. Before I knew it, the test was over. I hadn't finished, and once again, I'd failed. Up until now, that had been my MO.

But Mr. Evans saw deeper than most cared to look, and he knew what to do. He quieted my anxieties by giving me the final exam in a study lab, in a private cubicle. There was a clock, but not within view. The only yellow pencil was in my hand. He told me how long I had and what percentage I must attain in order to pass. Numbers and letters seemed to arrange themselves before my eyes; equations simplified themselves, or seemed to. It was magic. I turned in my paper and he graded it right then. I'd pulled a B.

Math still isn't my easiest subject, but now, when a problem seems a bit too difficult and I feel the anxiety starting to stir within, those old fears still simmering in my subconscious, I remember Mr. Evans. He came from somewhere in the South, Mississippi, I think. I can still hear his voice tinged with a slow, soft accent. I close my eyes and imagine a wide river meandering through the Delta, take a deep breath, and remind myself that, yes, I *can* do the math.

The Odyssey

By Christa Allan

One of the required ninth-grade readings is *The Odyssey*. Not all twenty-four books of it, of course. Those who determine selections in textbook anthologies tend to underestimate the endurance and curiosity of high school students. But that's a rant for another day.

Homer's epic poem, which consists of over 12,100 lines, covers the ten-year period following the Trojan War as the hero Odysseus makes his way home. Sly Odysseus was the one credited with the idea of using a huge wooden horse as a gift to the enemy, thus getting past Troy's city gates. That night, the horse's belly erupted, spilling Greek soldiers into Troy and wreaking destruction (hence the expression, "Beware of Greeks bearing gifts.").

So sometime during the reading of the excerpted portion in our textbook, the inevitable questions arose: "When's the test?" "Is this going to be on our exam?" "What do we need to know?" "Are we supposed to be able to spell all these names?"

All good questions—but ones I didn't yet have answers for.

How *could* I make it interesting, and what was the best way to assess their progress? I decided to cruise one of my favorite teacher blogs, Eduholic, by Emmet Rosenfeld, hoping for some inspiration. The teacher-gods were with me that day because I stumbled upon Emmet's "Play Odyssey" idea.

I had the kids form groups with the end goal of creating a game that would incorporate specific literary terms, plot points, and vocabulary from their reading. My twenty-three freshmen flung themselves into this idea with enthusiasm, intensity, and focus. What made my teacher-heart go thumpety-thump was eavesdropping on their conversations and the intelligent observations and questions they had, like "How many times did Athena really help Odysseus? How many men did he lose when the Polyphemus started brain-bashing his men? Let's use this vocabulary word because I think we need to know what this means, and don't you remember the story started in medias res?"

Each group chose a different approach. I watched them give and take within their groups, working to sort out who did what best, pushing even the reluctant and the cynical to action. The groups weren't in competition against one another. In fact, they helped one another by having a "play day" to test directions by playing their games. What was most remarkable to me is that not one time did anyone ask me about the grade for this project.

But enough of my observations. I wanted to share some of their reflections, because I'm incredibly proud of them and hope they are equally proud of their efforts.

Taylor: "This project was kind of crazy because this is English class, not the Parker Brother's Game Class. I also felt a sort of relief because I knew that this was going to be fun."

Amanda: "I learned you need to be patient with others. I learned more about the Odyssey by doing this project because I was no longer confused."

Hunter: "I learned how great something can turn out."

Hannah: "I feel accomplished."

Samantha: "I learned that the Odyssey has a great lesson: to be loyal to the ones you love."

Caitlyn: "I didn't really understand the book, but if you have to make a game from a book, you have to learn the book."

Katherine: "I learned if you're going to try to lead a group, it's extremely important to listen to the members' complaints and ideas."

Amy: "I learned that people who make games must be really smart."

Carson: "I learned that directions have to be specific in order for people to understand every detail."

Allie: "You have to get along with your group to actually get something done."

Matthew: "Everyone has to help for the project to be good."

Anne: "At first I didn't want to do an Odyssey game. I thought it was going to be hard and boring. Now that it's over, I enjoyed doing the game. It was fun, and it helped me understand the Odyssey better. I also learned that you have to put aside differences and work together."

Joel: "Making games isn't as easy as it looks."

Loreal: "The game-making helped me learn things I couldn't understand from the book because as you made the parts, you learned the material."

Ashley: "Making a game fun, yet educational can be tricky."

Carley: "Before the game, I didn't really pay attention to character names and vocabulary. After, I was forced to pay attention and think about what I was typing."

Alyssa: "I learned that working on a project with people is a very hard thing."

Mrs. Allan: "I learned to not underestimate my students' abilities to rise to the challenges set before them, and, sometimes, all I need to do is point them in the right direction, then get out of their way."

Miss Burns

By Susan Merson

Mrs. Von Kozlow checked for dirt under our fingernails and was known to make Charles Matella wear a piece of yellow twine through his belt loops to remind him to tell his mama that he had to wear a belt to school. Mrs. Greishammer drove a sporty red convertible Spitfire and circled the school every day with an extra rev, just to give the kids a little thrill. Miss Smith wore buckets of White Shoulders perfume under and between the many folds of her arms and stomach. But it was Miss Burns who captured my heart and set it free.

She was beautiful: big buck teeth, teeny blue eyes, leathery skin, and Kennedy-esque athleticism—all of it downright exotic in my world. Miss Burns went skiing, smoked, and laughed loudly, tossing her head back like a braying donkey. And Miss Burns got me. She looked right into my pudgy, Eastern European soul and located America.

My family was close—and loud. My father, a graduate of the school of hard knocks, was pounding at the American dream, and Mom was still not sure why everyone didn't take blintzes and gefilte fish to the school lunchroom. My aunts cawed at each other and poured themselves into girdles and corsets that kept their soft bodies sausaged and bulging at knee and bosom. The uncles swatted cigar smoke and argued about the price of school shoes for their growing families, admiring the fact that they had actually managed to put a roof over everybody's head. Nobody went for a jog or built things with their hands. That was for the goyim.

Mostly, America was for the other guys. Our family was our country, and we lived in the midst of blue-eyed blonds who tipped their hats but really couldn't be trusted at the grocery store. The message was "stay in the family circle or risk death." Until Miss Burns.

In our third-grade classroom, she introduced us to her best friend, a large African American woman who sang the blues and called us "God's chillun." Miss Maybelle worked as a nurse's aide in a nearby old folks home, but she sang for third-grade classes, apparently, and let us know about her cousins who lived in Mississippi where you couldn't yet drink from the same water fountain as your white neighbors. She hugged Miss Burns and gave her a kiss on the lips, right there in front of the blackboard.

Miss Burns made white frosted cupcakes the day Miss Maybelle came to class. "If you eat two cupcakes, two times a day, besides a bellyache, what do you get?" she asked, never missing the opportunity for a teachable moment.

And she believed in the natural world. While my own

home was spotlessly clean, the windows were always shut. Fresh flowers that dropped petals and animals that bore bugs were things from a muddy shtetl past, forever to be kept at bay. Miss Burns wore her hiking boots to class so she could show us how her footprints on the earth would leave a trail. We tracked her up and over boxes and under desks and finally into the cozy reading corner where we all took off our shoes and read about the talents of Indian trackers and how they showed us the way to the far side of our country.

One day she pinned an entire branch to the bulletin board.

"Keep your eye on this prize, everyone," she said as she smiled with her secret.

The stick was brown and dry, withered, and at the end of its life. It had a bumpy pouch, and I wondered why she would bring such a dead thing to our classroom.

"Don't judge a book by its cover or a person by the color of their skin," she cautioned us. "The strangest surprises begin again as a sunrise and patience will bear great fruit."

Miss Burns wasn't at school the next week. Mrs. Petrillo, our principal and substitute teacher, told us that Miss Burns had been in a skiing accident and had broken her leg. No one was sure when she would return.

My heart was broken, and my hand actually shook as I penned my get-well card on the lightly lined paper. Meanwhile, Mrs. Petrillo stuck to the book, but I couldn't hear her. All I heard was Miss Burns's laugh and the way she shortened my ethnic name to a one-syllable American moniker, naming me as someone more than who I was at home.

I felt as dry and flattened as that dead branch still pinned to our back bulletin board. If Miss Burns wasn't in class to show me the way out, I was stuck in my own circle forever, and I was already feeling its constraints.

We got the news a week later. Somehow, the broken leg got infected and Miss Burns grew so sick that she died. Actually died and went to heaven. Everyone had been asked to come to school a little early so Mrs. Petrillo could introduce our new teacher. The new woman was small, skinny, and bland. That's all I remember about her, but I do remember that when we first entered the classroom that morning, every desk was covered in snowy white balls of fluff with small seeds attached to them. The withered branch with the lumpy pod on the bulletin board had finally released its contents—delicate beauty released into the world from the scratchy boundaries that held it. And like those seeds born away on white feathered hope, we would all live to grow another day and plant our own good in the world. The wind blew through the window. Miss Burns urged us on.

The Hat

By Elynne Chaplik-Aleskow

It started as a typical first-class session of the new semester at Wright College in Chicago. Twenty-five faces were staring at me with the fear of college students who would prefer to be anywhere in the world other than in a communication class. As I looked back at them with all the empathy I could express, I asked that everyone wearing hats please remove them. Many looked confused—a generation unfamiliar with such etiquette—but the hats finally came off. Except for one young man's.

When I asked him directly, he answered "No." I was shocked but didn't show it. Not ten minutes into the session—and in front of new students—I was being challenged. How I handled this moment could determine semester survival. My semester survival.

The students were intently watching me and waiting. It was my move. I decided not to deal publicly with this challenge to my authority, so I asked to see the young man after class. His name was Mark and he looked least likely of all the students to express insubordination. He was slight in build, clean-cut with a pleasant face. He was not someone who stood out among the others. Yet he had said "no" to a directive from his new professor in front of new classmates on the first day of the new semester. There would be no choice; I had to convince him to do what the others were asked. He would have to back down.

After class, alone in my classroom, Mark and I faced each other. His eyes focused toward the floor. He wouldn't look at me as I spoke. His hat, the symbol of his defiance, still sat securely on his head.

"Mark," I said softly, "you must follow the rules of this class. Removing your hat demonstrates respect. Is there a reason you feel you must wear your hat? I'm willing to listen."

Mark lifted his eyes and looked into mine. "No," he answered. His look was empty. His tone was flat.

"Then you must remove it," I answered in my most professorial voice.

He did as I asked, and at that moment I recognized my challenge with this young man. He complied in removing his hat, but I hadn't reached him. I'd forced him, but I hadn't persuaded him.

Slowly throughout the semester, I felt a bond growing between Mark and me. Sometimes he'd even smile at my jokes and ask thoughtful questions in class. When I saw him in the hall, he would tip his hat. I didn't let him see me smile.

The final week of the semester Mark asked me to stay

after class. He had something to tell me, something he'd kept secret.

I'd come to know him as a gifted poet and hardworking writer and speaker. Harder than most perhaps, because Mark suffered from multiple sclerosis (MS), which had affected his coordination and vocal cords. Some days the class and I understood him better than others.

"Do you remember the first day of class when I refused to remove my hat?" he asked.

"Yes," I answered.

"Well, now I'd like to tell you why I did that. About a year ago I went to an open mic forum to read my poetry. They laughed at me."

"They what?" I asked, not wanting to believe what I was hearing.

"They laughed."

His speech was labored and painfully slow. "I was humiliated."

We were alone in my classroom and looked at each other through our tears.

"That first day of class I was trying to get you to throw me out. The course was required, but I didn't want to ever stand before an audience again and perform my writing. But you wouldn't give up on me. You wouldn't let me leave."

"You chose to stay, Mark," I answered softly.

For his final persuasive speech, Mark spoke on stem cell research funding. He passionately argued for our government to acknowledge that it is his quality of life they are ignoring and for his classmates to vote for legislators who would make the stem cell reality happen. Would it be soon enough for him, we all wondered?

After offering an articulate and informed argument, Mark walked with great difficulty to his visual aid, which was an empty white poster board. He asked his audience to give him one thing. Only one thing. He picked up a marker and with a shaking hand he wrote the word "Hope," one painstaking let-ter at a time.

A year after he'd completed my course, Mark came to my office to say hello. He proudly told me that students from our class would stop him in the hall and tell him that they would never forget his last speech. The MS was progressive and he was suffering, yet he looked happy and at peace with himself. He had formed a team in his name for the MS Walk each year and was trying to raise money to help himself and others through funding for research.

Three years later I received an e-mail from him. He wanted me to know that he was writing again, and that for the first time since he'd been traumatized by the experience, he again performed his poetry in front of an open mic at a Chicago club. He said he could never have done it without my course. In his last line he told me that he always wore his cherished hat.

The Power of One

By Abha Iyengar

Mathematics was a subject I could never fathom. And by the time I was in tenth grade, this lack of understanding began causing major problems. Visions of a bright-enough daughter being closed out of all good colleges plagued my parents.

My father couldn't fathom how I failed at math, belonging as I did to a family of mathematics lovers, so a tutor was assigned to help me. I think the tutor was as bored with the subject as I was. His attempts at teaching me resulted in my score plummeting further (yes, you can get 0 percent in math!), and he was sent off. I was glad to see him go, for the stress of learning from someone who doesn't know his subject is worse than trying to do it yourself.

The next tutor, a woman, was so caught up in the goings-on of her love affair that she was not the least interested in teaching me theorems or square roots. Yet she gave me stern looks that froze me, and then one day hit me in sheer exasperation. I complained to my father, and she was also sent packing.

My math scores hadn't improved, and we were back at square one.

So my father decided to teach me himself, for he was great with numbers. Within the week, though, both of us had had enough. His impatience with my slowness simmered at the surface, and my inability to comprehend his fast-paced calculations tired my brain. Luckily, he had to travel to Mumbai for a meeting, and after that, we never broached the subject of his teaching me again. He had given up on me, and I think my pillow was wet for many nights thereafter. Yet, my determination also grew stronger. I vowed I would learn.

I began to search high and low for someone to teach me math. While searching high, I looked up from the verandah— at my grandfather sitting on the first-floor terrace of our home. He was a history and Sanskrit professor. He sat reading a paper, and it suddenly struck me that he also loved mathematics, loved to teach, and was retired. I sprinted up the stairs two at a time and ran up to him, huffing and puffing. "*Dadaji*," I pleaded, "please teach me mathematics!" I fell at his feet because I'd been running so hard.

He looked up from the paper. "Of course," he said, "get your books right away."

Right away? I shook with shock, then quickly complied.

Gradually, I overcame my fear of numbers. I understood that while words have their place in expression, mathematical expressions carry their own weight in life. That if a thing can be measured, then its certain outcome can be ascertained.

Algorithms have their own rhythm. Sets are not unsettling. Theorems need no theorizing; they need to be understood.

I also began to enjoy solving numerical puzzles. Every time I solved a geometrical problem after applying a theorem, I wrote Q.E.D. (Quite Easily Done) with a flourish at the end, a smile lighting up my face. I began to enjoy finding the capacity of cylinders and the areas of cricket lawns. I was becoming a master at calculating and problem solving.

I started to realize the power of one—one right solution to a given problem.

How did this happen? My grandfather began by teaching me the basics. He was very involved and focused. He never worried about a phone call, wasn't busy with any work, and above all, he knew the subject. My earlier tutors had known the subject, too, yet had failed to teach me.

My grandfather taught me with patience, guiding me carefully, never deriding or ridiculing me in any way for my ignorance and mistakes. He was clearheaded, careful, and gentle in his guidance, never raising his voice or getting impatient. He took me slowly through the process of learning about numbers. Most of all, he transferred his love for them and their magical abilities to me. I was not afraid and grew increasingly passionate about mathematics.

My grandfather proved again the power of one—one right teacher over the wrong ones!

I aced my math paper for the first time within a month of my grandfather becoming my teacher. He taught me every day for an hour, sometimes longer, for six months. After that, I was confident enough to explore and handle the subject on my own. I didn't dread math anymore. In fact, I looked forward to the classes at school. My results went up dramatically—100 percent!

My parents were very happy—and relieved. Their visions changed from fearing I'd never succeed to dreaming about the best colleges for me.

When the student is ready, the teacher appears. I was ready to learn, to help myself, and so the teacher in my grandfather appeared for me. Q.E.D. All it took was the power of one— that one *ultimate* teacher.

READER/CUSTOMER CARE SURVEY

UHFG

We care about your opinions! Please take a moment to fill out our online Reader Survey at **http://survey.hcibooks.com.**
As a **"THANK YOU"** you will receive a **VALUABLE INSTANT COUPON** towards future book purchases
as well as a **SPECIAL GIFT** available only online! Or, you may mail this card back to us.

(PLEASE PRINT IN ALL CAPS)

First Name		MI.		Last Name	

Address				City	

State		Zip		Email	

1. Gender
- ❏ Female ❏ Male

2. Age
- ❏ 8 or younger
- ❏ 9-12   ❏ 13-16
- ❏ 17-20   ❏ 21-30
- ❏ 31+

3. Did you receive this book as a gift?
- ❏ Yes   ❏ No

4. Annual Household Income
- ❏ under $25,000
- ❏ $25,000 - $34,999
- ❏ $35,000 - $49,999
- ❏ $50,000 - $74,999
- ❏ over $75,000

5. What are the ages of the children living in your house?
- ❏ 0 - 14   ❏ 15+

6. Marital Status
- ❏ Single
- ❏ Married
- ❏ Divorced
- ❏ Widowed

7. How did you find out about the book?
(please choose one)
- ❏ Recommendation
- ❏ Store Display
- ❏ Online
- ❏ Catalog/Mailing
- ❏ Interview/Review

8. Where do you usually buy reading about the books?
(please choose one)
- ❏ Bookstore
- ❏ Online
- ❏ Book Club/Mail Order
- ❏ Price Club (Sam's Club, Costco's, etc.)
- ❏ Retail Store (Target, Wal-Mart, etc.)

9. What attracts you most to a book?
(please choose one)
- ❏ Title
- ❏ Cover Design
- ❏ Author
- ❏ Content

10. What subject do you enjoy reading about the most?
(please choose one)
- ❏ Parenting/Family
- ❏ Relationships
- ❏ Recovery/Addictions
- ❏ Health/Nutrition
- ❏ Christianity
- ❏ Spirituality/Inspiration
- ❏ Business Self-help
- ❏ Women's Issues
- ❏ Sports
- ❏ Pets

TAPE IN MIDDLE; DO NOT STAPLE

FOLD HERE

Comments

The **ULTIMATE** Series

That Downright Mean Coach

By Louis A. Hill, Jr.

I was new to all of it in 1944—to Oklahoma A&M, to the academic scene, to any sport participation, and to Coach Higgins. My aim was simple: to get in one semester of college before I turned eighteen and could finally volunteer to serve my country.

What I didn't figure on was Coach Higgins's shenanigans. Slowly but surely he was making my life miserable. It came to a head that hot, humid day at the track meet. To suit the coach, I had just finished running the two-miler against another college when he had me run the miler against them as well. Nearing the end of the miler, my legs turned to lead and sweat was running off me, stinging my eyes with salt that blurred my vision. To keep going, I eyed a grassy spot in the shade off of the end of the track. That's where I was going to lie down and not get up for hours.

I touched the finish line and turned toward that grassy shade when I heard Coach Higgins yell, "Hill! Hill, where you going? You're going to run the half-miler now. Come on!"

"I'm spent. I can't, Coach," I said, still heading for the shade.

"Sure you can," he said. "Now get out there and run!"

"Coach, I can't! I couldn't even *walk* a half mile right now."

Coach Higgins caught up with me and looked me straight in the eye. "Hill, you don't know *what* you can do! Now get out there and run!" With that, Coach Higgins pushed me onto the starting line for the half-miler. At that moment, I thought he was downright mean. I couldn't figure out why all of the other guys thought he was so great.

As the pistol fired, my exhausted legs propelled me upright mechanically and started pounding the track. Presently I pulled away and a group formed behind me. But the three front-runners were already a quarter of the track ahead of me! How ridiculous to keep running when I was this exhausted and had absolutely no chance to win! *Why not just quit running and go lie down on that inviting patch of green grass?* I asked myself. But I didn't dare.

Just then the coach did something despicable. He sent one of his stars to run along beside me on the sidelines and heckle me. That heckler kept yelling, "Louis, you better run faster or that bunch behind you is gonna catch up and pass you! You're falling behind! Come on!"

I'd yell back for him to shut up but he just got louder and louder as he saw he was making me mad. Somehow energized by anger, I found myself running faster and faster. It was impossible, like a miracle, that this figure burning up the track was *me*.

My legs, no longer exhausted, were pounding harder and

harder. As I neared the stands, people started yelling and cheering me on. I couldn't believe how light my legs suddenly felt. My feet were flying. The people in the stands jumped up and down, cheering. As I passed the finish line, I could almost reach out and touch the number three man.

I was close to collapsing, but Coach Higgins caught me, looked me right in the eye, and said, "If you'd *really* started running a few feet sooner, you could have come in third. Or you might have even won! You had no idea what you could do—right?"

I nodded.

"Never forget that!"

That's when it dawned on me that the coach was *not* downright mean.

I don't know if Coach Higgins could ever have made me a star runner had I not gone into the army. But I do know that what he taught me that day became a powerful influence in my life. When I faced difficult challenges as a company commander in the Philippines, as chairman of the Civil Engineering Department at Arizona State University, and finally as the dean of engineering at the University of Akron, I never sold myself short. When things got real tough, that "downright mean" coach's words came to mind: "You don't know *what* you can do . . . not until you give it your *all!*"

Old Crow

By Mary Cook

The Victorian school building stood out like a decaying tooth in the mouth of hell, surrounded as it was by the desolation of postwar Britain. But a dashing war hero was to lead me beyond the ruins.

Arundel Street Junior Mixed School was in the center of Portsmouth on the south coast of England. A major naval port, the city had lost about one-third of its homes and businesses to German bombs.

Alastair Crowley-Smith, my class teacher, was a man of many passions. And he had the talent to convey them to others. No dry academic, he lived and breathed whatever subject he was teaching at any one time. An ex–fighter pilot, he'd been shot down three times by enemy fire. I was going to marry him when I grew up. The fact that he was married with five children meant nothing to my eight-year-old mind. I referred privately to Mr. Crowley-Smith as "Old Crow."

Thoroughly steeped in the arts, he was an ardent admirer of Vincent van Gogh. He brought in a reproduction of the artist's *Sunflowers*. We painted sunflowers that looked like blobs of yellow paint. But then he told us the story of how van Gogh had gone mad and cut off part of his ear—stirring stuff for eight-year-olds. We felt inspired to paint sunflowers with fresh vigor. He collected fistfuls of bluebells, and we streaked our paper with the searing purple-blues we found in our pastel tins.

Another of Mr. Crowley-Smith's passions was archaeology. He devised a house system in which we were divided into teams of Romans, Normans, Saxons, and Vikings. One day he came into class carrying a brown paper bag containing numerous fragments of Roman pottery. When he asked who would like a piece to keep, thirty-plus hands shot toward the ceiling.

He walked around the room, placing a shard on each child's desk. I handled my fragment reverently out of respect for the toga-clad individual whose long-dead fingers had created the pot and decorated it with cross-hatching.

The next day we made Roman-style pots from modeling clay.

Mr. Crowley-Smith loved poetry and drama. A talented actor, he was a leading light in the Southsea Shakespeare acting troupe and drilled us in Shakespearean theater. He also introduced us to the traditional poetry of the Border Ballads. My favorite was Lord Randall, with its story of a young lord poisoned by his sweetheart. I particularly enjoyed intoning the chilling refrain: "Mother, make my bed soon, for I'm weary wi' hunting and fain would lie doon . . ."

In those days, the way you spoke mattered. If you let it be known you came from a poor background, you stayed poor. But Mr. Crowley-Smith raised our sights by giving us the social advantages that came with elocution lessons.

He also taught us that figures were important in everyday life, but I never mastered those. When he called on me in class to answer a math question, I was a rabbit caught in the glare of his headlights. No, make that head*light*—he rode a drop-handlebar gold racing bike. We children fought among ourselves for the honor of wheeling it into school.

In the unlikely event of his still being alive, Mr. Crowley-Smith would be proud to know that somewhere there is a moderately successful writer who was one of his "mixed juniors." I'd like to thank him for his valuable lessons. And though I suspect he knew it went with the territory, I'd apologize for dogging his footsteps with my puppylike devotion. I have a confession also—I still can't stand Shakespeare!

Uncommon Teachers, Unexpected Lessons

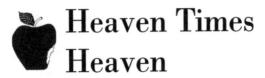

Heaven Times Heaven

By Cristy Trandahl

"Teacher! Teacher! Wanna play rock, paper, scissors? How 'bout freeze tag?" little Brian hollered as he tromped up my front steps. His chubby face glowed with the prospect of yet another victorious match.

"Rock, paper, scissors *after* multiplication facts," I conceded with a smile, pushing a plate of chocolate chip cookies toward the boy as he plopped down his backpack and jumped into his seat at my kitchen table. Of all my tutoring students, Brian was my favorite—and my most challenging.

Significant abuse and neglect by his biological mother had left the ten-year-old with permanent physical and cognitive limitations. Running was difficult. Writing, a challenge. Retaining simple mathematic algorithms could throw Brian (and me) into a fit. His social skills, while generally acceptable, still required tweaking: "Remember, Brian, we can't hug everybody we meet!" But this boy was resilient, bighearted, creative, and full of joy. The love given to him by his adoptive parents and biological sister helped Brian overcome insurmountable obstacles every day. He was main-streamed in class, and enjoyed many friends and hobbies.

This particular afternoon, a sunny May Monday, I was determined to help Brian conquer the "sevens" multiplication facts. "Okay, Buddy, here's a new one: seven times seven. It's a doubles, right? Seven, seven times . . . let's make a story out of it."

"Can there be boats in the story? Maybe chocolate chip cookies, too!" he suggested, reaching for a second helping.

"Sure . . . seven times seven . . . seven rhymes with heaven; so let's say heaven times heaven is boaty-line. That's seven times seven is forty-nine. When you see the number seven can you think of heaven? And in heaven you can ride in your boat with your fishing line anytime you want. So, 7 × 7 = 49!" On a flashcard, I diagrammed the problem with a picture of a boat and fishing line.

"Got it, teacher. Heaven times heaven is boaty-line. Heaven times heaven is boaty-line." As Brian repeated the prompt, I could almost see a little motor churning in his mind. I became encouraged. We were really making progress. Together, we could get through the sevens today, the eights next week . . . why, we'd triumph over fractions in no time!

"Can we play rock, paper, scissors now?" Brian pleaded, brown eyes twinkling. I sighed audibly. *We have multiplication facts to learn, and all he wants to do is play*, I mumbled to myself.

"One championship round of rock, paper, scissors, then it's back to the sevens," I relented with a smile. I won, six rounds to four. And got a hearty hug as a reward. After that tutoring session, I waved good-bye to Brian as he hobbled to his mom's waiting car. A little dejected, I assessed our progress for that day. Two hours of work, and my student mastered only four of the multiplication facts.

That evening, I confided to my husband, "It's so difficult trying to teach Brian the important things like mathematics when he's so excited about games and boats and playing outside. I'm trying so hard to be creative, but some things you just have to learn through repetition, repetition, repetition!"

For almost a year, I tutored Brian. We played slapjack spelling and crash-up math facts (he got to crash down a tower of blocks if he answered the multiplication problem correctly). He made me laugh with his jokes: "Teacher, what kind of teeth can you buy for a dollar? Buck teeth!" I baked cookies for him. He entertained my toddler with magic tricks. Then it was time for me to take a leave from tutoring to have my third baby. Another teacher would have the opportunity to tutor Brian until I could get a schedule running smoothly again.

That summer, while swimming, Brian drowned. I never saw that beautiful boy again. He had never learned how to reduce fractions, spell the word "beautiful," or locate the capital of Texas. Brian was just gone.

At Brian's funeral, scanning the hundreds of stunned faces filling the church, I marveled at the gift this little boy had been. So many people would miss his sweet smile, boundless energy, and determination.

As I left the church that day after Brian's service, wandering despondently toward my vehicle in the parking lot, I glanced up at the fair summer sky. Hundreds of balloons, bright and buoyant and boundless, hovered overhead, lifting toward heaven. "Heaven times heaven is boaty-line . . ."

"Can we play rock, paper, scissors, teacher?" "What kind of teeth can you buy for a dollar? Buck teeth!" Brian's jaunty voice floated in my mind like those soaring balloons.

And that's when I realized the truth about my teaching. The truth about life. While I had been drilling my special-needs student with facts, concerned that he learn the important things in life, he had, in fact, taught me what was important. In the grand scheme of things, it was not so vital for Brian to memorize the seven times table in one week flat. What was important is that we laughed. That we played. That together we sought out this thing called knowledge. In the process, we formed a relationship, however brief, that will now be brought with him to eternity.

At a little boy's funeral I discovered that love and joy were the most enduring lessons I could ever teach any of my students. For me to learn that lesson just took some . . . repetition.

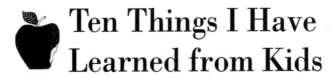

Ten Things I Have Learned from Kids

By Linda Kaullen Perkins

As a second-grade teacher of many years, my students have taught me a lot. You might be surprised to learn these ten unusual facts.

1. It is possible to wear shoes on the wrong feet all day and not realize it.
2. White liquid glue can explode. (Chances increase if the user or bystanders, within a mile radius, are wearing new clothes.)
3. The cleanest kids get head lice.
4. A new pencil can be sharpened every five minutes and last all day.
5. Mice, turtles, and snakes can escape from anything before the end of a school day.
6. All the points can be worn off new crayons in one day, all the crayons can be broken in two days, and every one of them can be gone in three days.

7. Children can walk around with small toys entangled in their hair for days without anyone noticing.

8. Family secrets can be revealed at show-and-tell in the blink of an eye.

9. The song "America" praises the unknown country of Tistletee. (Think about it—My *country Tistletee, Sweet land of liberty.*)

10. Paper jewelry made with love is much more valuable than gold.

His Joy Became My Joy

By Ellie Braun-Haley

I thought my patience as a teacher was exceptional until the day I took on a diverse and extraordinary class. Then the real test began.

I received a phone call from a lady who was looking for a private dance tutor to work with a young girl with developmental disabilities. The girl, I was told, had rhythm and loved music. I was a dance teacher with absolutely no training in working with people who were disabled, but something in me felt challenged, and I responded with a yes. I would soon learn teaching can be as trying and complex as learning.

One-on-one classes really deplete the energy of both teacher and student, so it didn't take long for me to realize I'd made a mistake and knew I needed to terminate the classes. I rang up the guardian of my student, intending to bow out gracefully, "You're right, she does have rhythm, but I feel she would do much better in a group setting."

I had no idea about the determination and tenacity of these caregivers. Not only would they not take no for an answer, but within a day, they returned my call and announced, "Okay, we have three more students for you!"

In a short time, I had thirty students. These were teens and adults up to the age of forty, all with developmental disabilities. Yet because I had no experience with this, I was the one feeling a bit handicapped. I approached a colleague at the college where I was teaching and asked to sign up for classes to learn more about disabilities.

His response was both revealing and surprising. "No, I wouldn't do that if I were you! If you come to my classes I'm going to tell you all of the things these individuals cannot do. But if you go forward and attempt to teach them what you know, with an expectation that they'll do it, many of them will succeed."

Since he was the expert, I decided to go forward without special classes. I soon came to realize that my students were like other new dancers. They had their own personalities, skills, and abilities. Each was unique. I had students who learned quickly and others who had "two left feet." There were some who challenged me with a vengeance to utilize my creative side.

When I didn't achieve progress with one method, I searched for new approaches. With Sara I needed to make a comparison with something familiar. Sara spent more time looking at her feet than at anything else in the room, and it took a number of classes, offering encouragement, for her to trust me. I could see she loved the music we were working with, yet nothing I did seemed to help her. On one occasion I had demonstrated the movement of an arm, and Sara looked up at me quite puzzled. I knew she wanted to move, yet it was as if I were speaking in a foreign tongue. Because she was afraid to make a mistake, she remained motionless.

"Sara, the movement is like a propeller on a small airplane," I told her.

Sara knew airplanes, and as she connected the idea of a propeller with her arms, she looked at me and slowly grinned. She became animated. Her arms moved and her feet followed. Sara began to dance.

The students cheered one another with each small success, so each new move learned was a victory for all of us. I think we all felt the emotion of Sara's success and then Stuart's.

Stuart was spirited and enthusiastic from his first day, but putting two moves together frustrated him because as hard as he tried, things seemed to get confused between his feet and his desire. Stuart would repeat the dance steps out loud with me, as if hoping his feet might be more encouraged by the sound of his voice. When most of the class moved to the right, Stuart looked alone and startled to be moving to the left. On a grapevine step that called for students to step behind and then in front, Stuart became tangled and fell. We all felt Stuart's disappointment.

The first time Stuart tasted success was a special moment for everyone. "I did it, I did it, I did it!" he repeated over and over, rejoicing to himself and all his classmates. Leaping around the room with tears in his eyes, Stuart provided a Kodak moment for everyone.

Michael presented an entirely different quandary. He had been in class for three months and never participated. In all that time, he never spoke. He didn't appear at all interested in what was going on around him. On one particular day I'd been teaching a partner dance to the class. We worked on it for weeks, and that day I said my usual, "Okay, everybody, choose a partner." I was startled to see Michael suddenly in front of me, his arms outstretched. I said incredulously, "Michael, you want to dance with me?"

Not only did he respond with a big yes, but he knew every move. I rejoiced at hearing him speak and then seeing him opposite me, proudly performing every step. Michael's response that day reminded me again that we all learn differently. During all those weeks when I thought Michael had been wasting his time on the sidelines, he'd been learning—in his own way, to the beat of his own drum.

My students taught me patience, and our relationship developed over the time we were together. I learned that sometimes one small achievement is really a most wondrous feat. And with Andrew I learned that things are not always as they seem.

When it came to Andrew I felt like a failure as a teacher. I searched for ways to reach him, to see some indication that he understood the instruction or that he liked something about the class. I didn't think I was succeeding. The pathways in

Andrew's brain did not always lead him to the same conclusions as others. He didn't communicate with me verbally. He never gave me eye contact nor did he give me any indication that he knew I was alive. He seemed to have little understanding that he was in a class and there were expectations. He sat a lot and nodded his head, making humming noises.

One day Andrew's parents met me downtown and told me they were so grateful I was teaching the class at the college. They said our class was the high point of their son's week. I was confused. How on earth could they tell Andrew liked the class? I believed they were merely being courteous. I continued to feel I had failed their son.

A week later, a blizzard held me up and I arrived later than usual. As I stepped out of my vehicle, I noticed Andrew and his caregiver just getting out of their car.

For the first time I saw ebullience in Andrew's face. He was beaming, and his body language indicated his anticipation. Finally I could see what his parents saw—an animated Andrew! He ran toward the building with eagerness. Because Andrew didn't generally display his emotions in the same way as others, I'd jumped to a conclusion that led me to berate myself.

He never danced, but I finally knew without a doubt there was something about the class that brought joy into Andrew's life, and I knew that snowy night, with tears and snowflakes on my cheeks, that Andrew's joy was my joy.

I'm so glad no one told me years earlier that my students

couldn't learn more and would never learn to dance. Because of one colleague's advice, I believed I could reach Sara and Michael and Stuart and Andrew and all the others who have come since. In accepting that first challenge many years ago, I opened a door into a new world. Bringing the joys of dance and movement to my students has blessed my life beyond measure and taught me things I might never have learned otherwise.

Cooperative Learning

By Rosemary McKinley

Even as an experienced teacher, I should have known that there could still be a first in my sixth-grade classroom. Somehow one early February a student locked a single toy handcuff on a diminutive girl named Crystal. The children had written skits in cooperative learning groups of four about a mystery that took place in ancient Rome. The students within each group had assigned different tasks to each other involving props and costumes. How handcuffs and ancient Rome go together, I will never know. But that's another story. In the meantime, Crystal was beginning to cry, and the boy was panicking, as was their teacher.

I had this group for eighty minutes before they moved on to their next class. Surely we would be able to resolve this problem. I calmed myself down and began to plan what our options were. Sixth-graders are very helpful so I asked for suggestions, partly because I was hoping someone had a solution and partly to keep them busy.

Two knowledgeable boys went to work to assess the cuffs.

They realized that the crank on the cuffs where the key went in was offtrack. This conclusion, while factual, didn't do much to alleviate the situation. The boys tried to line up the crank, to no avail. Next the perpetrator offered to call his mother to bring in another key to possibly open the cuffs. I sent him to the nearest pay phone with a pass and a quarter. The parent graciously appeared and tried the other key. No luck. In the meantime, both perpetrator and victim had tears running down their cheeks.

I, as the one in charge, was not remaining calm either. Time was moving along; thirty minutes had passed. I didn't want to call an administrator yet, so I asked for more suggestions from the class while the two boys continued to troubleshoot. In the meantime, I called the head custodian and asked him if he had any suggestions. He offered to cut the metal part off the child's tiny wrist. "It may hurt her," he warned.

When I relayed this message to Crystal and the entire class, they all responded with a vehement "No!"

Another ten minutes went by. The other twenty children gathered around the "cuff" couple. I decided to keep the children involved by asking them to write a story about what was happening in the classroom. No easy task.

I asked Crystal to come to the bathroom and see if we could use soap on her wrist and slide the cuffs off that way. I told her that it was up to her. We tried but at the last minute she didn't want me to yank the metal off. Large tears were running down one side of her face.

Time was moving along. I really didn't want to call the principal, but I had to remove the cuffs before the children were supposed to leave. I decided to call the custodial staff again. They would probably have the answer if they came to the room. When I peered down the hall I saw the short head custodian approaching, along with a very tall second one toting a large plumbing wrench and the matron carrying another tool. I heard the music theme from the western TV show *Bonanza* as they strode into my classroom. I knew the rescue was near.

When Crystal saw the wrench she became frightened, and her dark, almond eyes welled up again with tears. The head custodian told her not to worry as he produced a small screwdriver and proceeded to dismantle one half of the cuff. In the meantime, the clock was ticking and we were getting closer to class dismissal. As much as I didn't want to, I felt I had no choice but to call the principal's office and alert him.

After I called, Bill, the head custodian, was able to remove the cuff just as the principal and assistant principal walked in. Bill had saved the day. The children broke into spontaneous applause, and I nearly had to sit from relief.

The principal joked, "In the twenty-five years I've been in education, I've never seen anything like this!" The assistant principal nodded in agreement.

No formal teaching took place that day and the skits were postponed, but the children learned a valuable lesson in real-life cooperative learning.

The Power of a Leaf

By Diane Payne

There are times when I feel my role as a teacher is futile, and I seriously think about leaving the field.

One day, a colleague must have been feeling that same fatigue and asked if I'd teach something to her class using the leaves her mother had sent from Ohio. Since I'm a special education teacher, and my role is to hop from student to student, helping them with their projects in the classroom, I was eager to have a chance to stand in front of the class and actually teach.

Our school is near the Mexico border, and our desert had been unseasonably warm that fall. When the classroom teacher told her students how her mother had placed each leaf between the page of an old magazine so they'd be in good condition for them, these fifth-graders became incredibly silent, amazed that a woman they didn't know would send a package of leaves all the way from Ohio to Arizona just for them.

Watching them admire their leaves, I stood before the class wondering what we should do with them. In an hour they'd be leaving for lunch, and I'd be going to another class to work with different students. We had to do something special with these leaves, and it had to be something my special education students could do with their peers while I helped the entire class. Today I couldn't focus just on them. Japanese haiku suddenly seemed doable.

My autistic student seemed relieved to be counting out syllables on his fingers, turning words into a mathematical computation. Almost all the students in the class were Hispanic, and English was a second language, a language that often seems devoid of all romantic, lyrical elements. Knowing those leaves were a gift from their teacher's mother, the students held up their fingers and counted syllables, miraculously transforming bland English words into poetic messages.

At the end of the day, I was surprised to see them walking to their buses wearing the leaves proudly around their necks. They had finished decorating their yellow construction paper with yarn after lunch and were now displaying the leaves, which were surrounded by a haiku—so foreign, yet so intimate.

Watching the children appreciate the importance of such a simple gift revitalized both of us teachers who were feeling so futile. I still like to imagine how this mother in Ohio collected those leaves, immersed in peaceful happiness, knowing she'd be giving them to children living in a dry desert so far away from deciduous trees and unexpected gifts.

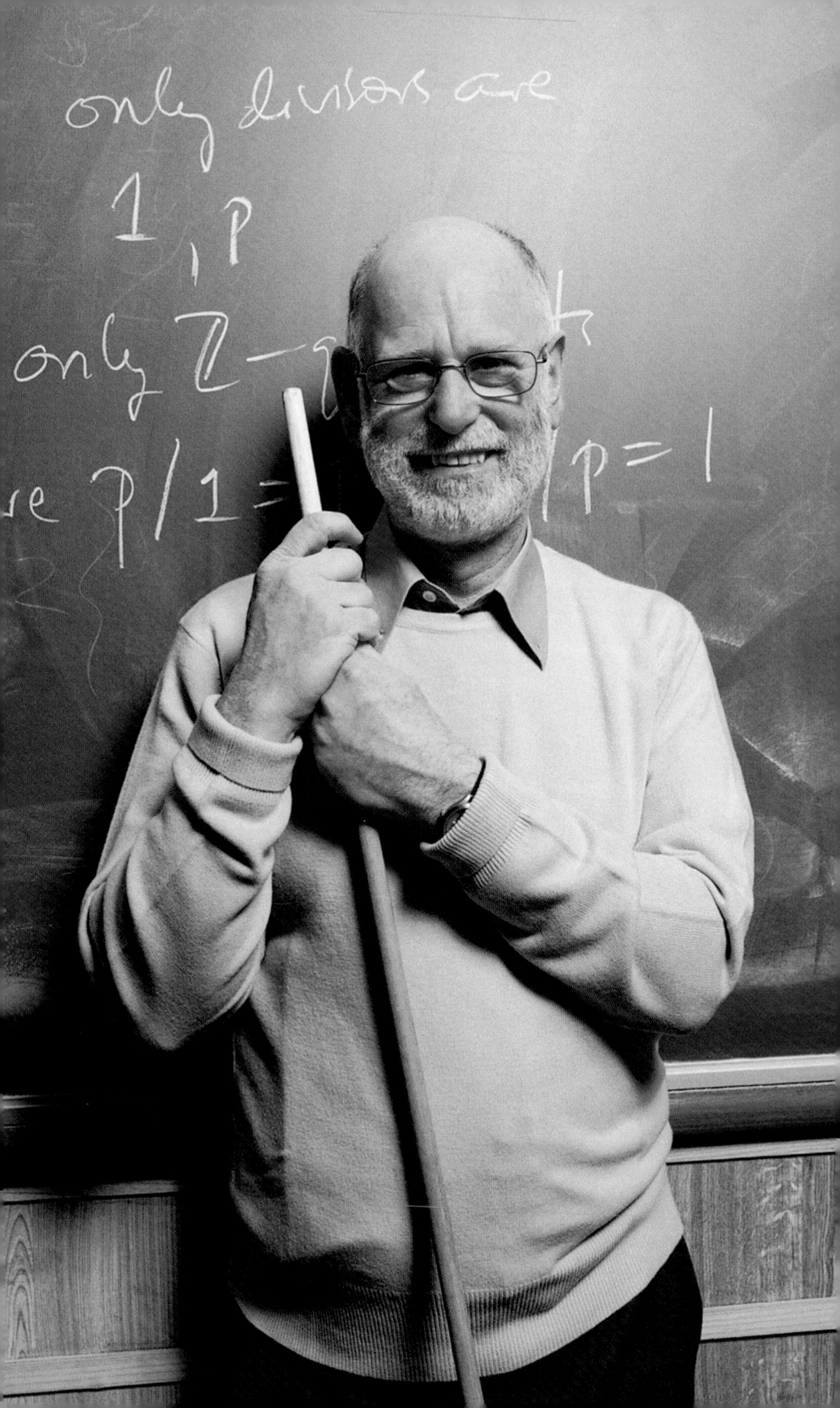
only divisors are
1, p

On Turkish Shores

By Elizabeth Phillips-Hershey

I think I was as nervous as he—this man who walked into the living room in a freshly pressed shirt, business slacks, and dark socks—this man with whom I'd spend two hours each weekday afternoon for a month.

"*Merhaba,*" Ismet said as his sister, Halide, my homestay hostess, introduced us.

"*Merhaba,*" I stuttered, my first attempt at a Turkish hello.

I had arrived in their Turkish seaside town with its eastern smells, head-scarved women, and men walking arm in arm the previous day. In the future, my husband and I planned to cruise Turkish shores on our sailboat, travel inland, and hopefully stay out of trouble. Learning the basics of the language would help us navigate, but more important, I believed that it might also open the country's soul to us. Ismet would be my teacher.

When I reflect upon my Turkish lessons, Ismet taught with two goals in mind: one was for me to learn the language; the other was that I begin to understand what it means to be Turkish. From the time I arrived, I felt the conflict in Turkey, a country that's approximately 98 percent Muslim, a country where Europe and Asia meet, where tradition and change have been at war since the establishment of the Republic of Turkey and the removal of Islam's control over its government by Mustafa Kemal Atatürk in 1923. And the debate continues.

Each afternoon, I opened the door of Halide's townhome to her brother. In Ismet strolled. He'd pause at the powder room, wash his hands, and then, with a flick of the wrist, smooth his hair. For me, it was Ismet's finely pressed exterior, without shoes, that represented the political and personal contradictions of Turkey. The veneer seemed impenetrable, but there were hints of something captivating and human.

We studied on Halide's balcony, where in the mornings I'd occasionally linger with her over a Turkish breakfast of bread, honey, olives, goat cheese, chopped cucumber, tomatoes, and tea. One rainy afternoon, Ismet and I huddled under the awning. I suggested we go indoors. He refused; he would not be alone with me inside the house. Ismet lived in a cosmopolitan area, had a university education, yet carried the family conventions in his heart. As my teacher, he'd stretched traditional male-female boundaries. And his response when the phone rang one afternoon was, "You answer it—it may be your husband."

What his sister left unspoken, Ismet explained. Over tea in a small tulip-shaped glass with three cubes of sugar, he shared stories about village life in their youth, how their parents traveled into town several times a year to shop. And when there was no more sugar for tea, they'd add preserves.

"My grandparents," he said, "emigrated from Caucasia near the Black Sea. My grandmother never learned Turkish; she spoke her native language, Abhaz. They brought their own religion to Turkey—ancient, isolated, similar to Greek mythology. My grandmother prayed to Ancadu [pronounced *Anjadu*]. It means Big Mother." God was feminine, the mother goddess, and they, along with other cultures that compose Turkey, merged their old worship with the new and became Muslim. I wondered whether his grandmother mourned the loss of the feminine power. I marvel now that I didn't ask Ismet. But maybe a man who always has a woman open the refrigerator door wouldn't understand?

Halide and Ismet's father visited Ismet during my homestay. Because his father still followed old traditions, he and Ismet's wife, Tamara, could not be in the same room. His father would walk into a room. Tamara would leave. She'd fix dinner and place it on the table. The men would eat without her. Tamara was not allowed to approach her father-in-law until one day, on this particular visit, he looked at her and said, "You may talk to me now."

One afternoon, Ismet and I rode into the center of town; unlike most Turkish men, he sat beside me. Our *dolmus*, which is a minibus and means "stuffed," jockeyed among cars, taxis, and scooters for road space. I clung to the bar in front of me as we charged down the dusty road lined with plastic bottles and grocery bags, among scraggly pine trees and ancient stone houses interspersed between red-tiled homes and hotels, veering around parked cars and children playing in the street. Over the clatter, I asked Ismet about Prime Minister Erdogan.

"He's Muslim," he mumbled.

"Isn't everyone?" I asked.

"You have to pray five times a day to be a Muslim. When I'm fifty and have retired, I'll have more time."

The closer we came to town where friends awaited, the more crowded the bus became and the farther Ismet edged away, until his right cheek hung off the seat.

I loved the sounds of the call to prayer, the muezzin's wail echoing through the narrow alleys, where women leaned over oil-burning cook pots frying *gozlemes*, a Turkish pancake. The smell of the goat cheese and spinach filling wafted through the streets. Men in knitted caps and woolen jackets with their prayer beads clicking sat silently on benches outside the mosques, staring at the hoards of tourists meandering by with tattooed balloon bellies or bikini tops and belly-button rings. I wondered what they thought of Western ways even as I rankled at their treatment of women . . . stuck upstairs in the stifling second level of the mosque on Fridays or trailing behind them, burdened with food and supplies from the market. I was as conflicted, I suspect, as they were.

One afternoon, as Ismet and I studied, he told how, after the earthquakes, when jobs were few and the younger people had relocated to Istanbul, the elderly men relaxed in the village center, drinking tea, smoking cigarettes, talking politics, and playing backgammon. Only when hungry would they return home to their wives, whose lives continued as before . . . cleaning, washing, shopping, and cooking.

"My parents," Ismet continued, "had little in common. Even today, men discuss politics and business; women converse about food, clothes, and family."

My sessions with Ismet were also politically spiced. He was a schoolteacher, but spoke as one accustomed to litigation and political debate. "Clearly, the U.S. made war on Iraq for oil," he lectured. "It would have been better if they said so from the beginning . . . be honest . . . don't play games." He leaned back in his chair and placed his arm on the balcony railing. "The U.S. is about power . . . always they have two goals—to change our culture and to teach their language."

I glanced away from Ismet and stared at the pink oleander framing the dirt road in front of the house. To support his claim, Ismet insisted that I learn Turkish history. In particular, one event especially troubled him: the Korean War. Turkish soldiers were sent to Korea to fight beside U.S. troops. Approximately 800 died. John Foster Dulles, secretary of state, publicly justified the use of Turkish soldiers, saying that they were *cok ucuza* ("very cheap"). It cost the United States twenty-three cents per soldier per day. Nazin Hikmet, a poet, wrote an angry poem in response. Ismet translated "The 23-Cent Soldier" on Halide's balcony. When he finished, he had tears in his eyes. I was humbled.

I see now that Ismet taught me more than just the

language; he offered a lens through which to view Turkish culture, Turkish people, Turkish life. Without his guidance, his introductions, his forcing me to view life through Turkish eyes, my education would have been incomplete at best, inaccurate at worst. I would have interpreted his world based on Western culture, based on my middle-class, privileged experiences, rather than his, perhaps misconstruing it, perhaps missing the essence of Turkey. I owe Ismet my thanks!

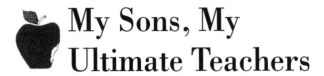

My Sons, My Ultimate Teachers

By Colleen Ferris Holz

My sister and I once discussed a reincarnation theory that souls return to life again and again, building each time on their learning about life and love. "That's disappointing," she said. "I'd want to stay in heaven enjoying eternity while sitting on a beach with a margarita in my hand. But you would probably love coming back for all that learning."

Yes and no. While it's true I love taking classes and learning from books, like many people I resist learning from actual life experiences, relying on a combination of procrastination and denial. This is why I dragged my feet in registering for a class that I, in my late twenties, knew would be my biggest challenge yet: parenthood. I waited eight years after getting married, despite my husband's readiness, because I dreaded the responsibility and all the sacrifices it would bring. I questioned whether I would make a good mother. Nevertheless, in November 2000, I met my first teacher, my son Hayden. His cofacilitator, Samuel, my second son, burst into the classroom in September 2003. My ultimate teachers were more than ready for their challenging student; both arrived on or before their due dates.

It's been "Extreme Learning" ever since. My children have turned me inside out. It was impossible to stay hidden from the world, burrowed among stacks of books, with those two rambunctious instructors around. They pulled me out from my inward focus and showed me a more active, creative, communal life. They have taxed my body (I have the chiropractor bills to prove it), they've stretched my mind, and most certainly enriched my soul. Some of the lessons have been quite mentally challenging, while others have been entertaining. They have taught a variety of subjects, some quite surprising.

The boys have instructed me in science, which was not one of my favorite subjects while growing up. Every day, questions are raised, hypotheses formed, and experiments are conducted. I'm constantly exercising creative thinking and finding new answers to problems. When Samuel was an infant, he wasn't actually a colicky baby, but did a great impression of one. The question of how to calm him was posed and theories were kicked around. We tested different solutions, from swaying while holding him, to "shhhing" him, to eventual success playing white noise on a radio.

Since then there have been all kinds of experiments, triggered by questions from the student: "What are the most effective ways to stop this negative behavior?" to teacher-generated queries: "What will happen if we add baking soda to apple juice?" or "How will Fruit Loops look after they're put in the freezer overnight?"

A great teacher stirs up curiosity. Hayden and Samuel's observations and questions have caused me to pause and really use my senses, to give greater consideration to my surroundings, things, and people.

My husband and I have learned tolerance and the art of negotiating. Our sons' anthropology classes have introduced us to the languages, cultures, and lifestyles of various beings who inhabit our home. The more memorable species include the brightly colored train cars that navigate on a mass transit system spanning the boys' bedroom, and the cloth, bean-filled creatures—enough to fill Noah's Ark twice—who talk to us in cartoon voices, begging that we adopt even more companions for them.

Most recently, we've become acquainted with a species made out of tiny blocks and connecting pieces. Some look like rectangular people, but most of them are robots. Often, their spaceship and weapon parts wind up scattered in our bed, our bathtub, and on our kitchen floor. Apparently giant feet do not threaten them! Some days my husband and I feel overpowered, despite our size. We've found that getting down on the floor at their level helps us negotiate with them. With our teachers' help, exploring these cultures teaches us greater playfulness and creativity.

Of course, none of these aforementioned classes could be mastered without the expanding understanding of philosophy and faith that I've learned from Hayden and Samuel. I'd always hoped to gain a greater appreciation for living in the moment, as Buddhism advocates. I presumed I was prepared for this course because of the prerequisites under my belt. I'd read books by Jon Kabat-Zinn and the Dalai Lama. I'd even taken a meditation course. It turned out I hadn't even scratched the surface. I now know that no book, no spiritual leader's advice, no workshop will teach me how to let go of obsessive worry (or at least keep it in check) and live more in the moment better than the practice of parenting. Hayden and Samuel have taught me about faith by presenting opportunities for slowing down, appreciating small blessings, and gaining a more positive (or at least imaginative) perspective. A permanent stain on the toy room carpet that tormented me was pronounced useful by Hayden, who said it served as a "mud pond for his construction site." My capacity for forgiveness and compassion has also increased tenfold since these instructors came into my life.

My resilience and persistence continually grows throughout every parenting battle. My boys continually chip away at the oppressive standards I hold tightly. Little by little they offer me the opportunity to lighten up and see humanity in all its glory and grief more clearly. I believe children remind us what is universal, and we all are a little kinder to others because of it.

During the day-to-day parenting struggles, I sometimes lose sight of the enlightened view Hayden and Samuel have worked to impart to me. This parenting course has indeed tested my wits at times. There is always plenty of wiping up to do from accidents and spills (some days I feel I should have brooms and rags attached to my body). The teacher-brothers' fights over toys or computer time have to be endured, as well as the failed discipline methods. Frustration with my teachers inevitably builds at times. I wonder if I will ever completely master patience and eliminate the need to raise my voice at them. Quiet time all to myself is always at a premium. But thankfully, the ultimate prerequisite for my sons' class is a willingness to learn. Their enduring lesson for me, no matter how great the challenge, is my appreciation for their instruction. With their help this soul is learning plenty about life and love—without having to be reincarnated.

Stop Poist

By Chris Bancells

Let's not beat around the bush. High school is an awful, bone-wrenching experience for most people. At no other time in your life are you so simultaneously trying to define yourself, while being meticulously judged by nearly everyone around you. The only safety is in cliques, groups of like-minded people who can offer a little protection through sheer numbers. The irony, of course, is that these cliques only serve to divide a school and make things worse. Every once in a while, though, things change. Sometimes, the cliques can forget their loudly declared differences and rally together behind an idea, a team, or, even more rarely, a single student.

It wasn't in the classroom that I met Austin Poist, but out on the cross-country course. I took over as head coach a year after the program had been neglected into oblivion, with Austin as the only runner willing to return. He was a quiet, obliging sophomore who still hung on to some bitterness that no one else had rejoined the team. I wasn't sure at first if he would stick around. He kept showing up though, and with his help I was able to cobble together a small team. Under normal circumstances, trying to convince teenagers that running is a sport and not a punishment is a tall order. When whole chunks of students have no idea your team ever existed, the task becomes downright mountainous. Nevertheless, our small group of new runners made it through that first year and dragged a few more with them into year two.

The second season we added something new to the program: enthusiasm. The new runners were excited to be there, even if the practices were hard and the team still small. The important part was that they were proud to be runners and said so, with Austin leading the charge. He was officially team captain now, and he lived and breathed running. He was always on the hunt for new recruits, always playing cheerleader for the newbies, and always out front. He was the fastest on the team by a long shot and dropped his times week after week. By the end of the season, he was pushing his way up the pack, putting our school's name in with the top contenders in the county. By season's end, he had qualified for the state meet with time to spare.

Having only been teaching at the school a few years, I had no idea how unprecedented this was. I had to ask around, since all the running records had been lost, but no one could remember ever having a cross-country runner qualify for states. From the get-go, I think I was more excited than Austin was, and I wanted to do something to make it all feel special. He was working harder than ever to get ready for the final meet. As

October ended, there were a lot of days when he and I were the only ones out on the practice fields. All of the other fall teams had either finished their play-offs or weren't good enough to go. Training to only the sounds of your own footsteps and a single voice shouting encouragement is harder than you can imagine, but he did it anyway.

The more he ran that year, the more Austin had become obsessed with Steve Prefontaine. One of America's best distance runners, "Pre" was so dominant that fans of his opponents took to wearing shirts that said "Stop Pre." When he still kept winning, Pre's fans started wearing the shirts ironically. It's one of the great pieces of running lore and was all the inspiration I needed.

A week or so before the state meet, I copied the stop sign design of the Pre shirt and changed it to "Stop Poist." I saved it as a computer file, attached it to an e-mail, and sent it out to the staff. I explained about the upcoming race, the sign, and asked the teachers who knew Austin to print out a copy and wear it as a button on Friday, the day before the meet. That was all. I thought it would be a nice confidence booster for him to see his teachers getting behind him. I had no idea what was coming.

"Stop Poist" was everywhere. Posters of all sizes materialized on the walls. Kids, most of whom I didn't know, flooded into my room, even during the middle of class, to get a copy of the button. They colored it in, put stickers on it, and added their own slogans. Even students who had never met him wanted to wear one. The band teacher printed out a huge version of it and had the whole band sign it (Austin was also on the drum line). It even migrated to a high school down the road; their cross-country team sent us a picture of them all holding the sign. Clique boundaries melted away as the whole school joined in the frenzy. Teachers, students, principals—it seemed like everywhere you looked, all you saw that week was "Stop Poist." Somehow, this lanky kid, who wasn't a part of any particular group, became something important to every group.

You know the saying "one rotten apple spoils the whole barrel"? That might have been our school motto. We had what amounted to a bunch of nice kids who often got overshadowed by a handful of mischief-makers. But for one short week, the students saw one of their own, one of the good guys, succeeding. Austin became a symbol of what our school could achieve. He became a hero.

In truth, I think the race was something of an anticlimax. Standing on the course with the other coaches, I realized that the most important thing for Austin and me had been just to make it there. Winning and losing were immaterial. What counted most about the whole experience, what was most memorable, was seeing the school come together. That's what heroes do best, they unify us, no matter when or where they appear. They inspire us and, in so doing, remind us that we aren't so different after all. Now, Austin didn't win the race, wasn't even close, but he ran a good one all the same. In the weeks and months that followed, things went back to normal at school. People went back to their routines, and a new sports season started. But when it came time to clean out lockers and classrooms in June, I smiled to see more than one "Stop Poist" sign reappear.

Teaching the World

By Kathryn Lay

hen my husband and I began dating, I knew that his heart's desire was to help people from around the world. I never dreamed we would teach the world from our own backyard or that our lives would be enriched in so many ways.

Nine years ago, my husband, Richard, began helping two students from our local college improve their English skills by meeting with them one night a week. We had worked with refugees before, helping them adjust to the country and becoming their friends. I was surprised at how much I enjoyed doing this and getting to know people from places I knew little about. And it seemed that the people we got to know felt comfortable with us.

It wasn't long before the students began telling others about this man who was helping them for free. Richard asked a friend to help by tutoring them during the day because Richard's full-time job as a teacher in the public school system kept him busy then.

More students came, and more help was needed. Soon he separated the classes into two groups according to their skills and needs. That eventually became four classes: low beginner, high beginner, intermediate, and advanced. Within six years, more than one hundred students from around the world were coming to learn or improve their English reading, writing, and cultural understanding.

Child care was another way to help these families. Our daughter became a part of a growing and changing group who babysat small children and helped the older ones with their homework.

By arranging for drivers, we were able to assist women and children who were anxious to learn English but lacked transportation. Every Monday and Tuesday night we watched as vans filled with eager students arrived—students who soon became friends.

As a homeschooling mom, and the wife of a teacher, I was thrilled that my daughter was able to learn more about other cultures in a more personal way than just reading about them. She danced at a Kurdish wedding, ate chicken feet with college students from China, and heard stories of escape from war from a Bosnian family who became some of our dearest friends.

As teachers and volunteers, we've seen students get better jobs, feel more comfortable in meeting and making American friends, and pass their citizenship tests to become a part of the new country they love.

"My teacher, my teacher," a woman yelled as we walked through a department store.

A young woman who had once been a student at the school ran up to us and grabbed my husband's hand.

"Oh teacher, it is so good to see you again. I tell you good news. Because of school, my English is better. I get the job at school for small children and help the teacher." She smiled as if she were holding the president's hand. "It was you, Mr. Lay. You taught me good. I have good job. My husband happy. My children proud. I thank you."

She turned to me and grabbed my hand. "Thank you, too. You become my friend. You show me library and take me to shop."

She hurried back to her family, who waved at us.

There are many times on Monday evenings when I've been tired from a day of homeschooling my daughter and would pre-fer to stay home. Richard comes home tired from a full day of teaching junior high kids. We've complained that we'd rather stay home and rest.

But, as a family, we go to our church every Monday and begin setting up classrooms, making copies of lessons, prepar-ing registration test materials, and making sure the other vol-unteer workers arrive and have the things they need to teach their students.

We are thankful for the many students who return and tell us about how the classes have made their lives better. And we are thankful for those who move away and cannot thank us, but who we know have been helped.

A student comes into the office and I show her to her class. Other students hug me or kiss my cheek, their clothing different from mine, their skin darker, their broken English spoken with a heavy accent. The new student, shy and nervous, is welcomed into the new class and finds a seat. Another lesson begins and both of our lives are changed through the experience.

Paying Dividends

By Michelle Mach

"See me after class." The note in red was scrawled at the top of my economics homework. I rolled my eyes. *Now what?* I didn't hate economics, but I certainly didn't love it either. Unfortunately, it was a required class. If I didn't take it—and pass—I wouldn't graduate from high school in June.

I glanced at the A scribbled below the note, then shoved the paper into a folder and began pushing my desk across the room. The teacher, Mr. Scarper, was enthusiastically rearranging the class into teams to track the progress of various stocks. "Think about your investments," he reminded us, as he strode around the room. "If you take care of them, they'll take care of you." I sighed and watched my team argue about whether it was a bull or bear market. In less than two months, I would graduate. And do what?

At the beginning of my senior year, I was sure I knew the answer—go to college and major in journalism. Everyone knew that's what you should do if you want to be a writer. So that fall I'd signed up to work on the school paper, a decision I soon regretted. My shyness made it difficult to interview people. I

didn't have any particular talent for writing headlines or sell-
ing ads. I couldn't work the computer and had trouble meeting
deadlines. My spelling was "a-trow-shush."

"Unacceptable," the journalism teacher had said, tapping
her index finger on my last story, the one I'd dashed off in
twenty minutes that morning with little thought given to
research or facts. "Completely unacceptable," she repeated.
She was right. I'd dreamed of being a writer ever since I was
thirteen when I published a poem in a local newspaper. But
when I dropped the newspaper class at the semester's end, I
knew I would never be paid for my writing. Even college
seemed uncertain. I didn't have talent or money—how could
I even think about college?

The bell finally rang. I grabbed my backpack and shuffled
to the front of the class with six other students, all clutching
our papers. We glanced at one another, trying to figure out
what we all had in common and trying to read the teacher's
expression behind his thick glasses. Mr. Scarper grinned and
clapped his hands together.

"You all did very well on this assignment. I'd like you to
take your essays home and rewrite them to meet the word limit.
Seven hundred and fifty words—not one word over."

"Why?"

I glanced at the male student behind me, relieved that
someone had the courage to ask the question lingering in my
mind. We already had our grades—good ones—and we were
supposed to do extra work?

Mr. Scarper pulled a piece of paper out of a notebook. "I'd like to enter these essays in this contest. Be sure to get them back to me by the end of the week."

He grinned, and I almost groaned aloud. Didn't I have enough homework already?

At home, I wrote and rewrote for several hours, trying to cut and reshape my essay to fit the contest theme, which asked us to explain how America needed to change in order to better the economy. I substituted short phrases for long ones and cut entire paragraphs. At the same time, I tried to keep my central idea that Americans could learn about economics by studying the Japanese car companies. I typed the final draft on the heavy black IBM Selectric that sat on the kitchen counter. Several hours later, I leaned back and proofread the essay. My neck and back ached. I had never worked so hard on writing before.

Later that spring, all the contest entrants from the district's five high schools were invited to a luncheon. The seven of us from economics crammed into Mr. Scarper's compact car, waving to the seven that were going with the journalism teacher.

The room began to fill with teenagers and teachers. As I clutched a sweaty glass of ice water, I began to feel a little hopeful. That is, until one of the girls in my economics class confided that her college boyfriend had helped her write her paper. "He's an econ major," she whispered. "At Berkeley."

Berkeley! I almost buried my head into my salad. It wasn't fair—I'd worked on my paper with no help from anyone, and now I didn't have a chance. I half listened to the speaker describe the various prizes and politely clapped as names were announced.

Then my name was called. Somehow I managed to get up, walk to the podium, and collect my certificate along with seven shares of bank stock. As I stumbled back to my seat, a student from the journalism group won a prize.

After the ceremony, when we filed out to the car, Mr. Scarper joked and waved to the journalism teacher. "One winner for each of us!" She smiled back, but I saw the confusion in her eyes. It was almost as if she didn't recognize me.

I couldn't blame her; soon I hardly recognized myself. During the last two months of my senior year, I became an essay-writing fool. Mr. Scarper encouraged me to enter another contest sponsored by the local bar association. I won second place and $1,500. Then I wrote an essay for a college scholarship and won that, too. When I graduated in June, I knew that there was more than one path, more than one way, to achieve your dreams.

Now, almost twenty years later, I still cash the quarterly dividend checks from those stocks. No financial advisor could ever persuade me to sell, even though I can easily earn twice the annual dividend with a single essay or article. While it's almost a cliché for writers to praise their English or journalism teachers for encouraging them, it no longer seems odd to me that it was my economics teacher who showed me the value of talent and hard work. After all, wasn't he the one who always stressed the importance of making good investments?

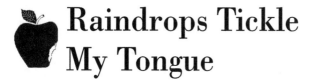

Raindrops Tickle My Tongue

By John J. Lesjack

I stood beside Vaughn and his wheelchair at the bus stop. Vaughn had a bone disease and couldn't walk. He had brittle bones, a round chest, and was undersized, but had happy eyes for everyone, even his teacher. His signed permission slip allowed him to go on a field trip with his fourth-grade class. He had never been on a field trip. I had never taken a handicapped person anywhere, much less on a daylong hike as part of our environmental studies. The thought was scary for me. I didn't see where he could gain anything special from an outdoor experience, but then I knew I'd gone into teaching because I had things to learn. Vaughn was an excellent reader and would have been safe in the library, but the principal overruled me.

The bus let us out at the nature center. One parent carried Vaughn off the bus and into the center. No chair for him today. Parents would rotate Vaughn from the back of one to another. Vaughn chatted and giggled with his classmates and parents while in the center and on the hikes. He traveled like a smiling backpack, and his smile touched my heart. The parents said he was so light he wasn't a problem. Of course, his friends wanted to carry him, too, but I said no. Vaughn had already experienced twenty-two broken bones and he was only ten years old. I wanted to keep all risks to a minimum.

Near the end of the day, a rain shower caught us out in the open on the coast. Our guide said we were close to the bridge to the lighthouse. Vaughn was on my back at that time, and I hurried everyone along so that we could all get inside the lighthouse and get dry. But when I saw the bridge, I stopped.

It was made of white slats held together by cables, and the cables stretched over a chasm between solid land and the rock formation on which the lighthouse was constructed. Beneath the bridge was a thousand-foot drop. I could see waves crashing on rocks through the slats.

My vertigo didn't allow me to walk on any bridge I could see through. Heights made my knees weak. But I was the teacher and couldn't allow my students to get wet, especially Vaughn. During my hesitation, Vaughn said, "Mr. Lesjack, I've never been in the rain before. This is neat." (He thought I'd stopped so he could enjoy the rain!)

Vaughn put his face toward the sky and opened his mouth. "Raindrops tickle my tongue," he giggled. Students around us began doing the same thing, giggling with him.

Averte oculus. The only Latin phrase I knew jumped into my mind. "Avert your eyes." In other words, if you don't see the problem, the problem doesn't exist. I decided that if I couldn't see the bridge, its height couldn't scare me. So, touching the railing with my arm, I shut my eyes and stepped into what my fear thought was infinity and beyond. When I finally felt the concrete floor of the lighthouse beneath my sneakers, I opened my eyes again.

Back in the classroom, Vaughn said to me, "Thank you for taking me on the field trip. Drinking those raindrops really did tickle my tongue." I smiled into his eyes and thought, *He helped me with my vertigo. Everyone had a good time, and I almost left him behind. I still have a lot to learn about this job.*

Nota bene: I retired in 1996 and never did learn it all.

New Teachers

Kenneth

By Samantha Ducloux Waltz

As I stood before my class of thirty-five fidgeting, adolescent English students my first day of teaching, I welcomed them, called roll, and filled out a seating chart. Then I passed out a list of class rules given to me by a veteran teacher. The students were to read and sign the rules, ranging from classroom procedures to homework policies. "This will tell the students what to expect and establish your authority right away," he explained. "It works every time."

The borrowed procedure went smoothly in my first two classes of ninth-graders. Now, most of my third-period juniors had their heads bent to the task. "Thank you for completing your work," I said in my brightest voice, and the rest of the students began to read or pretend to read the list of rules.

That is, everyone but Kenneth. Sullen-faced, he looked around the classroom. His eyes rested on the bulletin boards of bright yellow construction paper with white plastic lettering that I'd carefully prepared the day before, moved on to shelves of dictionaries and textbooks, passed over his classmates, looked at me briefly, then dropped to examine various marks scratched into his desk by decades of restless students. I'd noticed him when he first entered the room because of his suspicious, even angry demeanor. He was about ten years younger than I, a bit taller, and outweighed me by fifty pounds. Like a quarter of my students, he was African American.

I walked partway down the aisle toward his desk. "Could you please read the rules and sign them, Kenneth?" I asked quietly.

He looked at me, surprise in his eyes, perhaps because I'd called him by name. "Don't have a pencil."

I returned to my desk and got a pencil. "Please come with supplies tomorrow," I said and returned to the front of the room.

After several minutes I asked the students to finish up if they hadn't done so already and turn in their signed rules. Papers rustled and students whispered to each other as they passed them forward. Kenneth fidgeted, held the pencil I'd given him poised on his paper for a moment, then pushed pencil and paper to the corner of his desk.

"I'm happy to wait another minute for you, Kenneth," I said in my most encouraging tone.

He didn't move a finger toward his work.

I tried to sound confident and firm as I again moved toward his desk. "You need to do as I ask."

"No." He replied so softly I almost missed his response.

Every student watched us now. My breath caught in my chest and my knees threatened to buckle. Kenneth's ebony eyes met mine, hostile and determined.

"You need to do this assignment or go to the vice principal." I was determined, too. I didn't want to lose control of a
class on my very first day. I was also afraid.

"Fine." Kenneth sounded completely indifferent as he
gathered his books and ambled out.

My hands shook as I gathered the papers signed by the
other students, passed out textbooks and covers, and asked
everyone to write a paragraph on what they hoped to accom-
plish in class over the next year. I could have written Kenneth's
paragraph for him: disrupt the class, show up the teacher.
Would he be back the next day to create further problems?

I never quite regained my composure as I met my last two
classes, but I continued to pass out the lists of class rules and
everyone signed them without further incident. A number of
students actually seemed eager to learn, or at least eager to
please, and I silently blessed each of them. I looked forward to
teaching literature and writing, and to holding lively class discussions. I just needed to master this classroom-management
thing.

After school, as I was writing lesson plans at my desk, the
vice principal came into my room and eased himself into a
front-row student desk. "Have a minute?" he asked.

I felt embarrassed to have sent a student to him so soon, but
I was also relieved to see him. He could tell me whether Ken-
neth was returning the next day, and, if so, advise me on how
I could work with him.

"You're welcome to call me anytime you need a backup," the vice principal began, and my shoulders relaxed a little. Then he asked, "Would you be willing to have Kenneth back in class tomorrow? If not, we can put him into another English class."

A class with a good teacher, I thought. If I accepted Kenneth, he could resist my efforts every day for the rest of the year. If I didn't, I looked as incompetent as I felt. "Kenneth is a hard one," the vice principal said gently. "He's just up from the Deep South, living with an uncle. This is his third school in Los Angeles in less than a year. If he fails here, he's out of the system for good."

So it would be my fault if he got kicked out of school permanently. Just the challenge I needed to launch my teaching career.

"By the way, did you know Kenneth can't read or write?"

Can't read or write? The vice principal's words knocked me out of my own frightened space and into Kenneth's. Sympathy swelled in my heart for this boy caught in a system that promised him only humiliation and failure. Pride would prevent Kenneth from telling me in front of the other students that he couldn't read or write. He couldn't read my list of rules and sign it if he wanted to. No wonder he was hostile and angry.

I agreed to take Kenneth back. Hope rustled in my heart that I could make a difference for him. When he returned to class the next day, I whispered how sorry I was for the way I'd confronted him, and offered to work with him any day after school. He smiled tentatively and the anger in his eyes softened.

I wish I could say that I taught Kenneth to read and write that year. That he went on to graduate from high school and then college. The truth is that Kenneth and I had some successes. I still remember the pride shining in his face the day he showed me a card with his name that he'd printed in shop class. The shop teacher and I discussed other ways we could combine English assignments and shop projects to help him with his reading and writing.

But a few weeks into the school year Kenneth needed a schedule change to basic math, and, sadly, he was transferred to a different English class taught by a woman well known for her strict discipline and heart of ice. Evidently she pushed Kenneth until he cracked and threw a chair at her. Not that it was okay to throw a chair, but with no chance of success or even self-respect, what was he to do? So Kenneth was expelled from the entire school system and sent to a police academy for delinquents. I wondered if Miss Jones ever bothered to find out that he couldn't read or write.

Me? I tossed out that list of rules that provided no way for me to get to know the students before I laid on expectations. Every fall as soon as classes started I pored through student files in an effort to identify my students with special needs. I created a new list of class policies that had places for students to write in special concerns and to request after-school help. I gave

them out several days into the term. Mutual respect and indi-
vidualized curriculum became my focus rather than my personal authority.

Although my goal throughout several decades of teaching
was always to help my students, there were times when I simply
prayed that I wouldn't hurt the Kenneths.

The Rookie

By Todd Outcalt

A few months after my wife was diagnosed with breast cancer, she made the decision to pursue her lifelong goal of becoming a teacher. New careers and alternative paths are not uncommon after a cancer diagnosis, but my wife was particularly challenged by the prospect of leaving behind a lucrative pharmaceutical career for a lower-paying, entry-level position. Even so, she reminded me many times that this was her calling in life.

The challenges of becoming a teacher, however, were not just reserved for her work in the classroom, but involved our entire family. All of us in the family made sacrifices—especially our two teenagers, who frequently asked, "Where's Mom?" when they needed her assistance.

"Studying," was the usual answer. Or "Attending classes."

But as our family grew to accept Mom's commitment to education, we discovered benefits as well. Our teenagers were able, at times, to study side by side with their mother, and there were many times when they were inspired by the progress Mom was making in the classroom or by the excitement she found in conducting a scientific experiment in the kitchen. Graduation day in our house was unique in that our teenagers were able to witness their mother obtaining her second college diploma before either had enrolled in college. When my wife walked across the stage to receive her diploma, I noted that both of them were smiling—a subtle affirmation that they agreed with their mother's decision to teach.

"You can do it, too," was my wife's mantra to our children. "No matter what life hands you, don't give up on your goals and your dreams."

Of course, the teacher certification was not the end, but just the beginning. In the ensuing months there were job interviews, mounds of paperwork, and eventually a job offer. Mom had officially arrived, accepting a job as a middle-school science teacher.

Once again, our family was there to help make her classroom a special place. We rallied to help her decorate the homeroom. We carted in rocks for geology lessons, created models of rocket ships and planets for space lessons, and cut out interesting articles from old *National Geographic* magazines to display on the walls. We created charts, helped purchase large quantities of pencils and paper, and donated candy that could be used for classroom rewards. In essence, Mom's teaching became a family affair, and there was an excitement in the house when it came to learning.

"You know, it's tough to believe that Mom is a rookie

teacher," my son told me one day. "It seems like she's been doing this forever."

Indeed, the days before teaching did seem like another lifetime. Now it's difficult for us all to recall what life was like before teaching . . . and before that breast cancer diagnosis.

"Never give up on your dreams," is the primary lesson my wife tries to teach her students every day. "Be lifelong learners!" And sometimes, when those students hear my wife's story and the challenges she has overcome, they might find a bit more strength within themselves to believe that they can learn, too. Even from a rookie teacher.

Spelling Lesson

By Susan Stephenson

T o us, it seemed like an excellent idea at the time.

We taught first grade, Marcia Browning and I, both in our first year out of college, both keen to be creative in our approach to teaching. Our classrooms sat side by side under a huge gum tree in a rural Australian school. While cicadas droned outside our windows, we tried to instill a little fun into humdrum lessons.

One thing our kids loved was magic. They liked to spell words strung on macramé webs or pull numbers from a cauldron simmering over a cellophane fire. Australia doesn't have a big Halloween tradition, but that didn't stop us from decorating our classrooms with pumpkin heads, ghosts, and dangling skeletons.

One morning, Marcia found an enormous green tree frog on the windowsill. Immediately, I had what I thought was an excellent idea. The next day, we'd play a trick on Marcia's class. After school, we prepared my costume and practiced cackling.

At first, everything went according to plan. When my class visited the library, I swept into Marcia's classroom, clad in my old black dress with witchy tatters at the hem.

"Brwa-ha-ha!" I menaced Marcia's students with my glittering wand and straightened the black cardboard hat that tilted over my eyes. "I'm a witch and I've come to put a spell on your teacher."

"No you're not!" Emily jutted out her diminutive jaw. "You look just like Miss Ferguson. Only uglier." She tilted her head way back to examine my warty nose.

Marcia bit her lip and looked away. "Oh, please don't lock me in the storeroom, Witch."

I picked up my cue and shepherded her into the hall. The children followed. I pushed Marcia into the storeroom. There were gasps as I turned the key in the lock and chanted the spell.

"Bibbety-big and bibbety-bog, now your teacher becomes a frog!"

I flourished my wand a few more times to give Marcia time to complete our plan. With a final cackle, I threw open the storeroom door. The frog blinked at us from Marcia's abandoned, scarlet high heel shoes.

A hoarse sob burst the silence. I looked at the children's white faces. For the first time I wondered if we'd gone too far in our desire to add some drama to their lives. Was there such a thing as teachers being too creative?

Suddenly, I felt a hard kick to my ankle. I looked down.

"Give us back our teacher," screeched Emily.

"Yeah, bring her back!" The other children narrowed their eyes and moved closer.

"Er, Crickety-crick and crickety-crack, it's time for the teacher to come back."

Even the frog seemed unimpressed and blinked its bulging eyes at me. My step backward forced me up against the store-room wall. I could smell my own sweat and someone's banana sandwiches.

A footstep on the stairs saved me from the lynch mob. Marcia came in, reassuringly human.

"Sorry, had to visit the bathroom."

"Miss Browning!" Relief flooded the children's faces. Marcia hugged them and ushered them to their desks. They threw suspicious glares over their shoulders at the woebegone would-be witch.

Emily darted back and snatched up the frog. Bright blue eyes surrounded by clumps of wet eyelashes glared at me. If she'd been Medusa, I'd have statue status. She slammed the classroom door in my face, but not before she hissed, "Witch!"

At least, I think that's what she said.

Beginning Ideas

By Becky Kelley

Finally, there I was at my high school graduation. Sitting at the ceremony with my carefully curled brown hair squished flat by the canary yellow mortarboard cap, I listened respectfully to all of the official speeches. The whole time I was thinking, *Hurry, hurry, I need to get on with the rest of my life.* I didn't know what was going to happen or who I was going to be. I was only sure of one thing: teaching was not going to be a part of my future. My school years were past.

Fast-forward twenty-five years to August 23, 2005. As I stood before my first real college class teaching Foundations of Writing II, I wondered if they could hear my heart beating as loudly as I did. The room was bright white—ceiling, walls, floor, dry erase and smart boards—all so glossy I wanted to turn off some of the lights to lessen the glare and mask my shaking body.

I'd avoided college until the ripe age of thirty-five and even then majored in psychology. I could picture myself one-on-one, listening and solving problems, more like a logical math person than an English scholar. But of course, college is where you learn more about yourself and grow as a person through the knowledge you gain. I discovered that I liked literature and writing; finding the perfect phrasing to make my ideas and feelings clear left me as excited as a child taking off on a two-wheeler for the first time. I decided to add an English major to my psychology course load. After graduating with a double major, I followed the first instinct that led me to college and promptly began a doctorate of psychology program that summer. Two years into the program, things changed when I won a writing competition.

It took a month or two after winning the competition before I fully realized that psychology was not where I should be. I missed writing too much. Quitting that course of study, I enrolled in a master's program in literature with an emphasis on creative writing. Now, here I stood in front of my first college class, sweating like the air conditioning was broken. Foundations of Writing II is for people who don't feel like they're quite ready for an English 101 class, or for those who took a test that told them they needed improvement in spelling, subject-verb agreement, punctuation, sentence structure, and other writing fundamentals. I tried to sound confident in my ability to impart some wisdom.

I started off with roll call and asked what their goal was in community college. Most of them were teenagers fresh out of high school, but one student in particular caught my eye—and ear.

"Veronica Ridley," I said.

"Name's Ronni," a voice croaked. "Nobody calls me Veronica, sounds a little uptownish for me. I'm from here."

"What's your goal, Ronni?"

"I'm trying to get into the occupational therapy program."

Ronni was a nontraditional, first-time college student in her early forties. Her unevenly dyed red hair was speckled with gray and pulled back severely from her face. Short and stout, she had a stony voice that suggested many years of smoking. There was something about the look of her eyes and hard face that signaled a rough life. She reminded me of a woman truck driver I'd seen in a documentary.

The first teaching mistake I made happened on that first day. I'd invited our very knowledgeable librarian to give a presentation on research techniques. Her talk was very informative, but the students had absolutely no context in which to use this information; most had never seriously researched anything up to that point. During the hour-long demonstration, they mostly text messaged their friends while I tried to look like I was paying close attention and taking notes instead of drawing cartoon characters on my little yellow notepad. Class was limping off to a slow start.

After thanking the librarian and showing her out, I gave them a homework assignment. "I want you to write two one-page papers, one formal about a current event and one informal about something that happened in your childhood, and turn them in next week."

her just a bit harder each week. As I came to know Ronni, she smiled a little and even laughed a few times, a large throaty sound. She also began to tell me about her life filled with pain, drug addiction, brutal boyfriends, and brushes with the law. Even though we were born the same year, we had almost nothing in common. How could this worldly-wise person expect me to teach her anything?

In fact, I wasn't sure I could either. Despite all of her dedication, Ronni was still making simple mistakes in grammar a month after the midterm. It was then that I learned another lesson: take your problem to a higher power. In this case, it was the head of the English program, Dr. Betty Shiffman.

"I don't understand it," I told her one day over lunch. "Ronni is smart, works extra hard, and when I talk to her, I don't hear any of the mistakes she makes in her writing."

"Why don't you try having her read her papers into a tape recorder and then listen back to it while she reads the paper?"

Wow! I was blown away that such an uncomplicated idea might really be the answer for Ronni. I borrowed a tape recorder from the library just before our next session. When she arrived, I handed her one of her papers and said, "Read this into the microphone."

She took the paper in small hands with chewed fingernails and began to read. I was amazed that she didn't make the mistakes that I saw on the page, even paused where the commas should have been.

After she finished, I reversed the process by having her

listen to her reading while she looked at the paper. I saw a light come into her eyes. "Oh my God! You must think I'm an idiot."

"Of course not," I told her. "I knew you could figure it out yourself if I just found a way to show you. You're one smart cookie." If I didn't thoroughly believe that statement, then she made it true over the last few weeks of school. Another lesson learned: tell them what you want them to be so that they can try to become it.

The next time I read papers aloud, there was one that caused my throat to close up a little. "Excuse me," I said, "my allergies seem to be acting up." Before I even asked if the person wanted to be revealed, Ronni was nodding her head, wearing a big grin with her hand stretched as high as her five-foot frame would allow.

Instead of a final exam, I decided to have them write a formal argument paper. Ronni chose to compare women's salaries to men's in our state of Kentucky.

Every week when she showed up in the writing center, she had another bundle of research to show me. The librarian had become her ally as they searched through databases that might hold the articles and statistics that Ronni needed, and her curiosity grew with each new thing she learned on the subject.

When everyone turned in their final papers, I knew that I had to read Ronni's paper before I left for home. I wouldn't be able to sleep without knowing how she'd done.

When I got to the end of page one with no mistakes showing up, I started to smile. By the end of the six-page paper, I was beaming. She'd made a few common errors, but overall it was a stellar paper. I wanted to publish her first struggling paragraph from the beginning of class and that paper side by side in the newspaper for the world to see.

The last week of the semester, Ronni came in for her final session in the writing center, but instead of an assignment I just talked to her about how proud I was of her hard work. I could see the tears forming in her eyes.

"Am I embarrassing you?" I asked, afraid I'd hurt her feelings.

"No, it's just that I'm—I don't think anyone's ever said they were proud of me before," she whispered hoarsely. Then she took her 100 percent paper, slipped it into her binder, and slowly pulled out another neatly typewritten sheet. "I just wanted you to know," she said as she quickly got up and hurried out the door.

> Dear Mrs. Kelley:
> I just wanted to tell you how much I appreciate everything you've done for me this year. I don't know if I could have made it this semester without your help. Thank you.
> Veronica

Success as a new teacher! I'd meant something in someone's life and had learned so much myself. I was glad there was no one around to see the tears in my eyes, too.

The Promise

By Nancy Julien Kopp

I woke that fateful day immersed in anxiety and misery. How would I survive what lay ahead? It was 1959, my junior year in college, and I was studying to become a teacher.

I loved it, thrived in the preparations I was making to become a professional educator. Classes in English, psychology, reading methods, and more gave me no problems. What loomed ahead this awful day, however, made me shiver with fear.

No way out. I had to face the music, I told myself, as I dragged my reluctant body from the warm cocoon of blankets. Face the music? That was exactly what I had to do this morning. My churning stomach meant breakfast would be skipped today. Each tick of the clock brought me closer to disaster.

I donned coat and gloves, wrapped a scarf around my neck, and set out on legs that felt heavier with each step. For once, I didn't relish the walk across campus. Face the music? I shuddered as that simple phrase skipped through my mind once again. I journeyed slowly to the final exam in my "Music for the Elementary School" class—an exam with no paper and pencil. I might have done all right with a test like that. Instead, the professor would select any three songs of nine we had learned to play on the piano. The pieces were not concertos or études. These were children's songs, like "Mary Had a Little Lamb."

The professor explained the first week of class that we had to learn three groups of songs in three different keys. To be sure, we had all semester to do this, plenty of time to master them, he assured us. Music Department pianos were available for practice.

"Piece of cake," the girl next to me said. "Easy enough," another chirped as I glared at her.

"Cinch class," yet another said rolling her eyes to heaven.

I kept my silence, but the worry started right then and there. I had many talents, but music wasn't one of them. I liked to listen to it. I was able to appreciate it, but I couldn't learn to tap a triangle at the right time in third grade. I couldn't sing on key. I couldn't read the musical notes on a staff. No musical aptitude whatsoever. No musical education either.

I signed up for practice time several days each week all semester. Anyone nearby must have winced at my efforts. Lovely songs tripped off the fingers of other practicing pianists, and the music floated through the hallway.

I asked my roommate for help. After several sessions, she told me it was a hopeless cause and suggested I cry on the professor's shoulder, plead for mercy, or do something even more drastic. What that might be I was afraid to ask.

I did talk to the professor, pouring out my tale of woe. I explained that I was "musically handicapped."

"Have you put some effort into this?" he asked me. "Really put some work into learning to play these little songs on the piano?"

With tears threatening, I assured him I had. His answer was that I would do fine when the time came, and he strode out of the classroom after patting me on the shoulder.

Now, the day of my demise had arrived. I couldn't have feared execution anymore than I did this music exam.

The professor greeted me with a smile, rubbed his hands together, and said, "Well now, are we ready?"

I sank onto the bench and attempted to play the three songs he selected. He kindly picked what were probably the three easiest pieces, and I managed to butcher each one.

At the end of my futile performance, the professor beckoned me to his desk. He looked at me, started to speak, then stopped and wiped his hand across his forehead. "Nancy, this is what we're going to do. You've put in a great deal of effort, so I'll give you a C in this class on one condition."

"Anything," I answered.

"You must promise me that you will only teach in a school that also employs a music teacher!" he said and grinned at me.

With vast relief I made the promise.

I taught in more than one school district, but I always made sure it was one that had a music teacher. I'd watch with great admiration as music classes were conducted, as songs were played on pianos that these music teachers rolled from classroom to classroom each week. *What geniuses*, I thought, as fingers flew across keys.

To this day, the only musical thing I play is a CD player or radio. After all, a promise is meant to be honored.

The Substitute

By Diane Stark

I was teaching Mrs. Green's class, but I wasn't Mrs. Green. She'd just had a baby, and I was the twenty-two-year-old, fresh-out-of-college substitute covering her maternity leave. It was a second-grade class, and they were mine from spring break until the end of the year.

I was lucky; they were a sweet group of kids. Discipline problems were minimal. I counted my blessings that my first on-my-own teaching experience would be free of any major behavior problems. Talk about counting my eggs before they hatched!

During my second week of teaching, Latisha, a quiet girl, asked me when Mrs. Green was coming back. I informed her that Mrs. Green had to stay home and care for her baby. "She's not coming back at all? But I loved her! She was nicer than you are," the girl protested. A more experienced, and, dare I say, kinder teacher would have patiently explained that Mrs. Green cared for her too, but her baby needed her. I, on the other hand, simply said, "Well, she's not coming back, and I'm here now."

That afternoon, Latisha interrupted my lesson twice to ask the other children if they thought I was mean. I'd never had any trouble with her before and I was surprised by the rude outbursts.

As the days went on, Latisha seemed to be *trying* to make me angry. Anytime I asked her to do anything, she refused. She constantly talked back and never turned in her homework. She was disrespectful to me and encouraged the other children to act the same way. I knew I had to take action or deal with the impending mutiny.

I asked Latisha to eat lunch in the classroom with me. Of course, she had a smart remark, but I saw the look of curiosity in her eyes. We sat down and I said, "Latisha, you and I have a problem. We need to work this out because I'm going to be your teacher for the rest of the year."

"No, you're not," she said. "You're going to leave us, just like Mrs. Green did."

"Mrs. Green left because she has to care for her baby. She still cares about you and the other kids. But she has to be with her baby now," I explained patiently.

"Why aren't you going to leave?" she asked.

"Because it's my job to be your teacher. Do you want me to leave?"

"No," she answered in a small voice. "No, I don't want you to leave, but I know you will anyway."

"No, I won't, Latisha. I'm going to be your teacher from now on."

"Don't lie to me. All grown-ups leave," she spat out bitterly. Tears were beginning to form in her eyes. I was stunned. This child, who'd nearly made me cry several times, was now welling up in front of me.

"Please, Latisha, tell me why you're so upset," I almost begged.

She stared at me for a full minute and then answered, "Everyone leaves me. As soon as I love someone, they're gone. I don't even remember my dad. He left my mom when I was a baby. Now my mom always has tons of boyfriends, but none of them stay very long either. Most of them, I'm glad when they move out." Latisha said all of this on a single breath. She looked down at her feet like she wished she hadn't told me.

"And now Mrs. Green is gone, too," I finished for her. The child nodded and flung herself at me. Without either of us realizing it, she was sitting in my lap, sobbing. My heart broke for her. At eight years old, she'd already dealt with abandonment repeatedly. Who could blame her for her behavior?

When her cries subsided, she pulled away from me, embarrassed. She got up and sat back down in her own chair. Her tears had created rivulets down her dirty face. She stared at the floor, waiting for me to speak. Eventually, I said gently, "Latisha, I'm going to be your teacher for the rest of the year. No matter how you act, I'm not going anywhere." I reached out to wipe a tear from her cheek and added, "I promise I won't leave you."

I stood up to retrieve the box of tissues from my desk, but

when I turned around, the girl was gone.

I wasn't sure what to think of Latisha's disappearing act, but after our lunch together her behavior improved dramatically. As time went on, I saw a different child in Latisha. I saw a little girl who desperately needed someone to care about her. I was determined to be that person.

A few weeks later, there was an article in our city's newspaper that harshly criticized our school district. It's a large inner-city district, and it receives negative press for many reasons, most often because of our poor performance on standardized tests. I read the article to the class and let them respond to it. Most of them were outraged that anyone would "knock" their school. They seemed to take the criticism personally. I asked them to write letters to the newspaper in response to the article. The children relished the opportunity. Most wrote things like, "Our school is great and you don't know what you're talking about." They read their letters aloud to the class and high-fived one another for standing up for their school. Latisha didn't turn in a letter, but I decided to let it go. I photocopied the other students' letters and proudly sent the originals to the newspaper.

On the last day of school, I let the class watch the movie *Space Jam* as a treat. While the credits rolled, each and every child sang "I Believe I Can Fly," the movie's theme song. I had tears in my eyes and a lump in my throat while I listened to them. I told them never to forget that. Each one of them really could "fly" through life, making their dreams come true.

At the end of the day, each child hugged me good-bye. When Latisha hugged me, she handed me a folded piece of paper. It was filthy and wrinkled, but I smiled and thanked her. When everyone was gone, I opened that paper and found myself in tears once again.

It was the assignment I'd given several weeks ago, asking the children to write a letter to the newspaper. Latisha hadn't turned one in, and I'd assumed she hadn't done it. But here it was in my hands. This is what she'd written:

Dear *Indianapolis Star*,

You need to stop writing bad things about our school. We are a good school with good teachers who care about kids. I had two teachers this year. One had to leave to have a baby, but a new teacher came, and she didn't leave. Not even when I was really bad. Please write something good about teachers who let kids cry all over their pretty clothes.

Sincerely, Latisha

That was my first class. Now, more than a decade later, I can only recall about half of those twenty-three students. But I will remember Latisha forever. That little girl taught me that the best teachers aren't the ones who know the most. They're the ones who care the most.

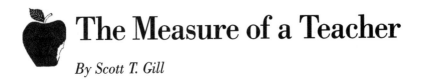

The Measure of a Teacher

By Scott T. Gill

"This is the Middle School English and Language Arts Content Exam for those of you who aspire to teach," the instructor said. "We need more good teachers out there, so, good luck. You may open your exam booklet and begin."

I stared at the test packet held together by a little red sticker. My future lay on the desk, bound to a ninety-question exam—the measurement of my ability to teach English. Anxiety washed over me like a tidal wave. What if I don't remember everything? What if I fail? What if I don't measure up? I hadn't felt this way since high school. Not since the first time I encountered Mrs. Vowell.

Linda Vowell was the new teacher on campus, and I had her for eleventh-grade literature and composition. My friends and I snickered that a lady named "Vowell" would be teaching English. We were going to have some fun with that name. Then the door slammed and a lady entered. She swaggered, not with the air of conceit, but with the confidence of an army general—her heels echoing on the hard floor as she moved across the room.

"I'm Mrs. Vowell and this is English. I want you to listen to exactly how we'll do things in here," she commanded. Her eyes were green, like jade, and I was mesmerized by their brightness. She hammered away at each point on the syllabus, barely taking a breath, "When you write, and you *will* write, you'll write well. One misspelled word will be an F; one run-on sentence, F; a fragment, F." I was slain—dead in the water. Out of all of the teachers, I was stuck with General George Patton. This was the teacher who all kids feared, the embodiment of those boarding-school caricatures found all throughout literature. I was sure I wouldn't measure up.

However, the following days showed not the language tyrant I dreaded, but a determined teacher, passionate about the great stories of old. Her passion was contagious. Whether it was the psychological journey of Dostoevsky's *Crime and Punishment*, the Old English of *Beowulf*, or her personal favorite, William Shakespeare, Mrs. Vowell set the room on fire. My friends and I devoured Shakespeare—Old English and all—from *Hamlet*, to *Macbeth*, to *Julius Caesar*. We read and wrote and thought and memorized, but most of all, we changed. We'd entered the class as a band of stooges, having once published a "Looker List" ranking every girl in school from fox to fatty, but now we were gentlemen of thought, budding scholars who debated texts and their impact. When I entered college, I breezed through every composition, each paper a mere trifle compared to the ones in high school English.

Yet, as my friends moved on through life and lessons, mine had only just begun with Mrs. Vowell. Angie (my high school sweetheart) and I kept in touch with our English master and even met her family. Her husband, Jeff, was a good man—the quintessential strong, silent type. They had two boys who, like all little guys, were full of energy and fun. Little did we know that these visits would turn into the greatest class we'd ever take.

We went to their home, ate dinner, and talked into the night about college and the future, and eventually the conversations turned to lessons on love, marriage, and the meaning of life. Once Angie and I were engaged, we doubled-dated with the Vowells, discussing everything from sex to family and faith. We learned about keeping romance in our relationship and fidelity when feelings faltered. Linda (that was hard to say) and Jeff became our mentors and counselors, but more than that, they became our friends. On June 6, 1992, Angie and I "graduated," standing before family and friends and vowing before God, "Till death do us part." As Linda played the piano and Jeff ran the video, we took our "finals" and began our new life together. After sixteen years of marriage and four beautiful children, we are truly thankful for the lessons learned in that final class.

As I stared at the exam booklet, still feeling anxious, I realized that it was no determiner of my capabilities but merely the government's way of telling the taxpayer that I'm qualified. A ninety-question exam is hardly the measurement of a teacher; that is only determined by the impact on a life. Who knows what Linda Vowell made on her content exam? She had such great literary knowledge that she probably did well. As far as impact, however, she was off the charts. When I look into my wife's eyes, hug my children, or write a story, her prints are everywhere. That's the true measure of a teacher.

I took the exam, opened it, and started to work, because when I finished, the greater task lay before me.

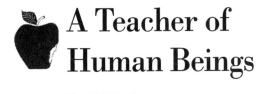

A Teacher of Human Beings

By Val Muller

I n ninth grade, I had an earth science teacher who'd been teaching since my mom was a high school student. He's my most memorable teacher because of his passion—not for earth science necessarily, but for his interest in the general enlightenment of his students. He had a T-shirt he wore occasionally that said "Books Change Lives." Each time he wore it, he told an anecdote about someone he knew whose life had been changed by a book. For me, a future English major sitting in the science wing, this action brought him to life. It showed me that he cared about more than just lunar cycles or the reason for solar eclipses; he cared about us. He treated us like people—not as just his job, as many other teachers tended to do. I knew if I ever had a problem in class, he was someone who could help. Though at the time I hadn't consciously planned on being a teacher later in life, his passion was something that stayed with me.

There are other teachers whose passion inspired me over the years. My first-grade teacher fostered a love of poetry among the entire class; I can still recite with passion Oliver Herford's "I Heard a Bird Sing," and it still warms me on dark December days. And there are others: my second-grade teacher who encouraged me to pursue writing; my elementary school and high school violin instructor, who in his spare time taught students how to build elaborate sets for school musicals; a student teacher I had in English who spent her after-school hours helping us produce a film version of Edgar Allan Poe's most famous scenes. Their dedication to their students and their passion for their subjects showed me they cared and inspired me to try my best.

Years later, after somehow choosing to become a teacher myself, I wondered what was wrong with me! My mom, probably the most passionate teacher I've ever known, would come home from work absolutely floating. She had countless stories of ways she inspired her students, or times when she paused during a lesson for a "teachable moment" about a memorable life lesson. When I called to order a bridesmaid dress at a local wedding shop, the shop owner recognized my last name as that of a teacher she'd had years earlier who helped teach her English. Sure enough, she remembered my mom, and Mom remembered her as a former student who had been an excellent tailor and dreamed of owning her own dress shop. My mother teaches adult education, and even today, she still gets a call every Christmas Eve from a student she taught two years before I was even born! At the end of the phone call, her eyes are always brimming with happy tears.

Compare that to my first year of teaching high school; all I wanted to do was speed up the three-digit countdown of calendar days until June's graduation. I wondered why the students were so averse to *The Crucible* or why they couldn't appreciate the imagery in Jonathan Edwards's fiery Puritan sermons. Well educated in American literature, I wondered, as I sat on my towering literary pedestal, why my students preferred to stay below and talk about video games, movies, or iPods. Weren't they interested in joining my crusade against comma splices and bad grammar? As we progressed through American literary history, some followed along hesitantly, a handful with interest, but most were apathetic or even confrontational about the material. I watched with horror as Anne Bradstreet, Patrick Henry, Mark Twain, and Kate Chopin took a backseat to World of Warcraft, text messaging, and the latest Hollywood blockbuster. I was alone on my pedestal, a precarious tower standing high above a sea swarming with student apathy, indifference, and day-to-day concerns. How long could I last?

It didn't take long for me to realize that, like my earth science teacher, my violin instructor, my English teacher, and my mother, I wasn't supposed to be primarily a teacher of literature. More important, I was a teacher of students. I started taking an interest in their interests, encouraging them to link the literary greats to film, television, and even video games. I imagined some of my college English professors cringing as I skipped a full-on examination of poetic allusions for a more creative, reader-response approach, allowing students to connect literature to their own lives. But I was reaching my students and making a difference.

This past year, teaching a small remediation class, I got very close to a group of struggling students. We worked hard on the skills they'd need to pass their state-mandated tests, but more importantly, they felt comfortable talking to me about their frustrations—both in and out of school. I watched their confidence levels grow as we developed a true bond. After the state testing was finished, they were no longer required to come to me for help—yet they still did. They brought not only their English assignments, but their history, science, and yes—even algebra! They said they felt comfortable around me because, unlike some of their other teachers, I treated them like people, not just my job. Now where had I heard that before?

Now that I've reached this epiphany, I've abandoned my literary pedestal and am finally combining my passion for literature with my passion for helping students. They're now with me on a ship that we're learning to navigate together. And it's well stocked. In addition to works of literature, I have students writing their own Ben Franklin–style aphorisms, penning creative narratives from the point-of-view of characters in the stories we read, and performing character-based talk shows about our current novel. I see students enthusiastically producing projects they're likely to remember years into the future.

It works out much better this way, for teaching is only effective if students are engaged. After all, it's hard to sail a ship when you're all by yourself.

Teaching by Example

Picture-Perfect

By D. B. Zane

Gabriel lost his recess privilege before nine o'clock each day. By the time I joined the second-grade classroom as a new aide, he had been diagnosed with ADHD.

"The school told the parents to get him tested," the teacher, Mrs. Benson, explained. "Don't know why we bothered. His parents refuse to medicate him, and the school is not sticking with its policy of following through or kicking him out." She seemed exasperated.

The problems weren't only in the classroom. Out on the playground, Gabriel played too rough. One day, he pushed a student so hard that her arm broke when she fell. The girl's parents were forgiving and nonaccusatory. "We would just like the boy to apologize," the mother told me.

Unfortunately, Gabriel's parents, blinders firmly in place, chose to accept only their son's version of events; the opportunity for teaching responsibility was lost, and a week of being benched during recesses did nothing to make Gabriel connect his overreactions to their natural consequences. Now the only discipline

Mrs. Benson had was to threaten a visit to the principal's office.

I sympathized with Mrs. Benson and her burnout. However, I wondered if we could find a way to provide more positive reinforcements. She did give out reward tickets, but only during afternoon circle time. My fingers itched to pass them out in the morning during reading groups and seat work.

Each day, I searched for an opportunity to praise Gabriel and the other students. He needed some positive feedback for even the slightest good behavior and appropriate choice. The day Mrs. Benson was out sick, I used those tickets as motivators.

"Thank you, Amy, for staying on task," I said gently, placing a ticket on her desk next to her work. Kids paid attention when they saw me slipping tickets to several more students. The class straightened up in no time.

Finally, for a brief moment, Gabriel sat, not biting his raw cuticles, not talking, and looking attentive.

"Look. I got a ticket! My first ticket," he waved it around gleefully.

I bit my tongue and allowed a moment of murmurs and whooping. It was already January and this was his first ticket? Certainly he could be afforded a few seconds to celebrate.

The next day, Mrs. Benson was back and the class returned to its normal routine—either attempt to behave or risk losing recess.

Timidly, I tried to share with Mrs. Benson the success of using more rewards rather than threatening punishments. "Oh, yes, I wholeheartedly agree. That's why those tickets are a vital part of my system." In vain, I continued to search for opportunities to reward Gabriel and the other students.

Then another opportunity arose.

"I've been called to an emergency meeting," Mrs. Benson informed me after lunch one day. "Here." She handed me a stack of papers to distribute.

Dutifully, I distributed the exercise and gave instructions. All too quickly, the class—most of it anyway—completed the work. I faced thirty-seven students, eager for learning or other diversions.

"Why don't we work on this?" I said more to myself than the class, grabbing a dusty pile of papers that had been on Mrs. Benson's desk since before I'd arrived at the school. I gave copies of the blank map of California to the class. Although the detailed geography was more appropriate for fourth grade, I hoped to create a combined art and geography lesson. Mrs. Benson had once commented that she'd been meaning to get to that map all year, but just never found enough time for social studies.

Step by step, I showed the students how to divide the state into its different regions (coastal, desert, valley, mountains). Then we created a key, deciding as a class what color to use for each section.

"Yellow for the desert," one girl suggested.

"What color is a valley?" they asked. After a brief explanation, we agreed to use green. One precocious student suggested, "Purple mountain majesties, like the song."

I used whiteboard markers to color in my hand-drawn map on the board as a model and then put the students to work labeling and coloring their own maps.

Mrs. Benson returned as they completed the lesson. While they cleaned up their crayons and turned in their papers, I explained the impromptu assignment.

"Great idea," she said. "Pick one or two as examples to show the class and post them on the bulletin board." So, while she took charge once again, I reviewed all thirty-seven papers.

It was disheartening. I thought I was a reasonably good teacher. I'd walked around the room to make sure the students were following along. I'd completed each step on the board as we went. Yet I could find no adequate examples. Many students had scribbled in each area rather than coloring carefully. Others created their own patterns of colors within the state outline that had nothing to do with California's geography. Lowering my standards, I consoled myself. These were only second-graders after all.

Then, nearly at the end of the stack, I found it. The paper was labeled, color-coded, and neatly colored. It was the perfect example—the only one. I couldn't wait for Mrs. Benson to finish her lesson so I could share it with the class.

"Mrs. Benson has asked me to select one of your papers for display in the classroom," I announced. "I found one work of art that was exceptional." I held it up for all to see. "See how neatly he colored each section?"

"Wow," the class muttered in awe.

"Whose is it?" several students asked without raising their hands.

Out of the corner of my eye I saw Mrs. Benson's jaw drop when I answered. However, I kept my eyes focused on the joy emitting from one special boy's face. "This paper belongs to Gabriel."

Tomaida's Treasure

By Jill Sunshine

Some students write a sentence in my life; they come, they sit, they say, "Have a good summer" at the end of the year. Some students write a paragraph in my life; they participate with passion in class, they take risks, they send me e-mail updates about college life.

But in the metaphorical book of my life as a teacher, a few special students from Malawi, where I served in the United States Peace Corps, held the proverbial pen and helped me write entire chapters. Wakala helped me pen the chapter entitled "Kill them with kindness." Mphatso held my hand as I wrote "Be brave in the face of unjust authority." Anthony walked me through "Swallow your pride and prove yourself with positive action." Although I was the one perpetually covered in chalk, they were the ones teaching me how to be a better teacher and a better person. Tomaida was, and still is, a chief penholder; she is the voice inside of me telling me I can do the impossible.

A small trading center without electricity or running water

served as the setting where I first earned the title of teacher, a title I took home with me as I continue to teach in the United States. After leaving this trading center, I dreamed every day for five years of returning. With the money my husband and I received for our wedding, we were able to purchase two plane tickets bound for Africa. We decided it was time my husband met some of the people who had molded me into the woman he married.

My husband and I arrived at dusk with our backpacks and no place to stay. There had not been time to write letters to inform anyone of our visit, but I felt confident that my former home would prove hospitable. We went into the store that had once been my hangout for playing Scrabble. When the grocer, a good friend of mine named Mapopa, realized who I was, he immediately called my former student Tomaida from his cell phone. So much had changed; Mapopa and Tomaida now owned mobile phones. However, hearing Tomaida's eager, "Madame, I am coming," made me realize that the important elements remained the same. The happiness in Tomaida's voice still filled my being with pure joy.

Within minutes, Tomaida showed up. She was dressed nicely in addition to owning a mobile phone. Obviously, this woman whom I'd taught five years prior was employed. She and I drank each other in, laughing at the fact that we were together again.

Tomaida had always been a star. She was in Form 4 (the equivalent of senior year) the first year that I taught. Unfortunately, she did not pass the frighteningly difficult Malawi

School Certificate Exam. Only one girl did, and only eleven students of our fifty passed that year.

Not passing the test rendered Tomaida's schoolwork null and void. Normally, that would indicate it was time to go home, get married, and procreate, but Tomaida had no inclination for normalcy. The next year, she was in my Form 4 class again, convinced that she would earn a certificate.

Tomaida's tenacity impressed me. A secondary school education is not free in Malawi. School fees are expensive, and having the gumption to use them two years in a row for a seemingly impossible task spoke volumes about her determination to earn an education.

When I was preparing to leave Malawi, I worked with Tomaida and generous friends and family from home to secure her a scholarship with the Elfrida Kumwenda Girls Scholarship Fund. Peace Corps volunteers had created the fund in honor of one of our Malawian trainers who had suddenly passed away. I knew that Tomaida was scheduled to take a typing course when I left.

The course was clearly successful, and although Tomaida had not passed the Malawi School Certificate Exam after two years in Form 4, her training from the scholarship had earned her a job with the Katete AIDS Project and later a computer job in the Katete Rural Hospital.

That week, my husband and I met Tomaida at her job. Seeing her smiling behind her computer, showing me what she did every day, filled me with pride. After a tour of the hospital, she invited us over for dinner to eat sima, cornmeal porridge, which is the staple food of Malawi. Throughout the week, more and more of my former students popped up, walking proverbs for how life should be lived. Mapopa, the grocer, had room for us in his home and happily housed us during our entire visit. I also saw Roger. He was hanging onto the back end of a truck that suddenly plowed through the village streets. Our eyes met. Although we hadn't seen each other in five years, he shouted, "Good evening, Madame Watson!" and continued to ride along, as though it were perfectly natural for me to be there. He taught me that a teacher/student relationship is timeless.

We saw Zikwe. He approached us as we walked around the market.

"I believe you are owing me a goat," he told my husband.

My husband's first thought was of the goat's head plunked next to the roasting meat for sale and wondered if this young man was trying to get us to pay for a snack. Zikwe saw his confusion and explained.

"You see, this one is my sister, and in our country, the bride's family is compensated by the groom. So, you are owing me a goat." He then burst into laughter, and we realized it was a joke. Zikwe's lesson: teachers are part of the family.

We also found Patrick, still strumming the same guitar he'd made out of a gas can, and still singing his one-hit wonder "The Killer Disease." This upbeat song with a serious message about HIV/AIDS that Patrick performed at many variety shows epitomized my view of Malawi: upbeat in absolutely any situation. With Patrick's help, my husband learned to play the four-stringed guitar, and they played and sang together in front of the video camera. Patrick's lessons were twofold: when life gives you garbage, create beautiful music, and when life gives you adversity, smile.

I was relieved and happy that my husband was so popular with my Malawian friends, colleagues, and students. This third family that needed to approve our marriage—my Malawian village—finally had the opportunity to authorize our relationship.

Later at Tomaida's house, my husband got his first taste of sima, which most Malawians eat for lunch and dinner every day. Afterward, we dipped our hands into a bowl of water to wash up, and I realized it was time to walk back under the African sky bejeweled with stars. I was sad to leave Tomaida's home and was thinking how much I would miss her when she came back in, holding folded-up papers like treasures.

By the light of a kerosene lamp, she unfolded them to show me her certificate from bookkeeping school and her Malawi School Certificate of Education. I expected to see the former, but the latter baffled me. How could she possibly have earned that after failing two years in a row? She explained that she went to night school after finishing the typing course, and she had finally passed the test. Tomaida's lesson: Believe in yourself enough to reach for seemingly unattainable goals. You will reach them if you believe you can.

Malawi was the greatest school I ever attended, and my

students were my most impressive teachers. They sacrificed so much for the chance to receive an education. Some walked far distances to school, others self-boarded because no schools were located close enough to home, and all paid school fees. And while they worked hard at their own educations, they simultaneously provided their teacher with one she would treasure as much as a hard-earned certificate.

Thanks to Tomaida, I will reach for goals despite the mirage of impossibility. Thanks to all my students in Malawi, I have a profound appreciation for education, life, and the infinite possibilities they provide.

In Training

By Cynthia M. Hamond

My daughter, Renee, and her family had just moved into an older home that they had restored, and we were unpacking boxes on the third floor. The early spring glee of neighborhood children released from the constriction of their winter confinement floated through the open window on the breeze.

My four-year-old grandson, Adam, yelled up from the sidewalk. "Daddy's home!" This moment of reconnection was the highlight of both their days.

I heard Matt, my son-in-law, getting Adam's bike out of the garage. Biking is more than a weekend pleasure to Matt. He bikes to work even in the coldest of weather. He and my daughter have biked all through Europe, Mexico, and the United States, usually with their two children in tow. Matt even volunteers on the board of Two Wheel View, a nonprofit organization that promotes world understanding by taking young people on bike trips to other countries to experience the culture and to interact with the people.

". . . and I think we can take the training wheels off," I heard Adam say. I looked down from the window and watched Matt adjust Adam's bike helmet.

"Well, son, when you feel ready, we'll do that. Let's go, Buddy."

Adam straddled his bike, lifted his foot to the pedal, and shoved off with Matt riding beside him. A few moments later there was a terrified scream. It froze my heart and sent me running to the windows to see where it was coming from.

My daughter just kept emptying her box.

The next scream jolted me into action.

"Renee, don't you hear that? Some child is in terrible trouble. Grab your cell phone," I yelled as I started for the stairs.

"Mom, everything's fine," Renee said.

I could hear Matt's voice, "It's okay. You'll be okay."

Another screech. Didn't she understand? Was she in denial? Adam was hurt. He needed our help, and he needed it now!

"Mom," Renee said, "that's just Adam riding his bike."

What? Was she kidding? Now I was really confused. "Did Matt take off the training wheels?"

"No, this happens every night. Adam wants to ride his bike, so Matt helps him. He does great until he has to turn a corner." I stared at her for a moment, processing the information. Then we both laughed.

Adam's siren squeal continued as he rounded each corner.

And following it were Matt's encouraging words, calmly coaching his son. "Here it comes, Adam. Slow down. Now make the turn. Turn the handle, Buddy. Turn, turn. A little more. There you go. Use the curb as your guide. Good job."

Around and around the block they went, Adam screaming, Matt alongside him pump for pump, patiently teaching his son.

"I'm proud of you, Buddy," I heard him say as he and Adam came up the driveway.

"Maybe tomorrow we'll take my training wheels off, right Daddy?" Adam asked.

"Buddy, training wheels are okay. It means you're in training, like an athlete. That's how I learned to ride a bike."

"Really, Daddy? I'm in training? I want to ride my bike as good as you."

"You ride your bike as good as I did when I was your age."

Matt ruffled Adam's hair as they started toward the house. Adam burst through the doorway and ran up all three flights of stairs. He was flushed with the success he had found in his father's words.

"Grandma, I can ride my bike as good as my dad. He trained me." He hugged my legs.

Matt came up the last step. I couldn't resist an over-the-head-of-the-grandchild grandma wink, along with a little mother-in-law laugh. "Yes, Adam, I heard you ride your bike, and you are as good as your daddy. He's a good trainer."

I hugged Adam, "And that's how I know that someday, you'll be a dad as good as your daddy."

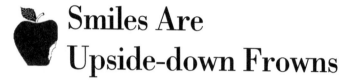

Smiles Are
Upside-down Frowns

By Lois Greene Stone

Did she teach me how to die or how to live?

The cancerous invaders in my sister Carole's stomach were surgically removed. Signet ring carcinoma. Sounded ominous, especially coming soon after heart bypass surgery. Well, she was diabetic, and her heart, therefore, aged quicker, right? I'd pushed aside that our father died from a heart attack at age forty-five, and our mother's line didn't fare too well with her first of several heart attacks at fifty, then heart bypass surgery years later. But what made Carole, who lived alone, gutsy enough to go through chemo and radiation for nine months? How did she manage? I wondered, from my house 3,000 miles away, what she must have been thinking as solution dripped into her body and beams blasted tissue? Then cancer returned to what was left of her stomach anyway. Was she bitter? Why not?

I began to write down childhood happenings, almost as if I were hoping it would keep her alive. Our wet wool snowsuits used to smell awful, and we wore Breton hats with grosgrain streamers or very large satin hair bows handmade by our mother. Our bicycles had balloon tires and no speeds. No. Too general. I began again.

At sixteen, she was part of a summer-stock professional group in Bucks County, Pennsylvania; I couldn't believe her talent for acting, singing, dancing. There she was onstage with people I'd seen in movies, and she was actually part of their cast! I'd write about that. Would that make her sad since she didn't pursue it but became a wife and stay-at-home mother instead, so common for the time to either have a career or motherhood? I began again.

Might be funny to hear about her long braids being stuck in an inkwell in elementary school. The awful boy in the desk behind would take her thick hair and dab the ends in ink. My short, silky, thin blond strands could never even be braided!

Or maybe, instead, I could write about how I felt back then. I was sarcastic when she was bossy. I pretended to dislike her. I wondered why she bit her nails. I never complimented her incredible aqua-colored eyes. Sometimes, just to assert myself, I walked a completely separate avenue from the regular route to elementary school, just so I wouldn't be with her. Even when we took our radium-covered jewelry into dark closets during World War II, I remarked that mine had a brighter glow. Listening to the *Battle of the Baritones* on the radio, if she liked Crosby's voice, then I picked Sinatra's, or vice versa. And when we played "Rather," if she said she'd rather have cancer than polio (the always-used question in that game) because at least she'd be dead and not in an iron lung, I picked the opposite. In an iron lung. Not Dead. But she now has cancer!

I began again, because I wasn't remembering what we shared, but rather the stupid sibling situation so common in families. Competition. I thought I was strong, she weak. Little did I realize she'd become a hero with strength almost unbelievable to me now.

As adults we didn't communicate for a very long time. Why? What had been so serious to separate us? So silly that neither of us even remembered the trigger. But we always, even then, had a common denominator: snapshots of our parents in our individual wallets.

None of this was what I really wanted to write. Just another "smoke screen." I was running out of time to be "real." I knew she was wheelchair-bound, had survived yet another cancer surgery, then heart failure, then pulmonary emboli. How? My husband and older son are internists and our daughter is a registered nurse; I know that weakened patients with heart sections closing, even though bypassed and not able to be stented, do not generally survive failure or emboli. How did she? With her optimism, she told me through the phone lines—that *she loves life, has had no choice as to what was handed her, only what to do with it.* Frail, extremely thin from disease, her body and her spirits were incompatible. I used to pretend I could conquer anything, playing out my self-assurance often at her expense, but she is the strong one. She is the role model. I went back to my pen and paper.

What would I want to tell her if this were to be our last conversation? That's what I ought to write: how her hand felt when she took mine to cross a wide boulevard each day for kindergarten; how she looked as a bride in satin and lace; how excited I was when she let me actually hold her firstborn, not afraid I'd drop the infant; and the big-sister way she touched my just-turned-twenty-year-old face at our father's gravesite. I'd say how much I really loved her, and how I'd liked her next to me when we pulled the radishes we'd planted in our victory garden. Her zest for living was there as a child when she'd take the sled to a higher hill; I'd only do that on a dare. She did it to better see her surroundings. She's gone through life this same way, and still did in early December 2004. I put the pen down. Tears were staining the paper.

It's hard to sort out what to omit or present to anyone. She was always looking forward. Even that December, when the permanent feeding tube was surgically implanted in what was left of her stomach, weeks after another operation to search for more cancer hiding within, she merely mentioned that she'd miss eating.

Maybe I'll just appreciate that philosophy and write down what she's offering all who know her. I won't pry about tears she suppresses or fears she must have in the silence of night, and I'll let her know she's an amazing woman to accept the ravages of her afflictions and still find humor with each.

I telephoned her after a five-hundred-mile car trip in constant rain and dense fog. My husband and I had just returned from spending New Year's with my daughter and her family, and I wanted to let my sister know of my safe arrival. Pneumonia and infection were ravaging her fragile body, but her clear words to me on January 3, 2005, were "Thank God you're home safely. I love you."

"Comfort Measures Only" were initiated that night, with a drip to keep her hydrated, medicines administered to control pain, and an oxygen mask. "Hearing is the last to go," my daughter, the nurse, told me. I telephoned my niece at the hospital and had her put the phone to my sister's ear. I continued the life-oriented charade and said I hadn't spoken to her that day and wanted to update her on the family's goings-on. She was conscious and responded, but with the oxygen mask, I couldn't make out specific words. No matter. Over the next few days, so many times she seemed to be unconscious from heavy medication to quiet her brain's intact thoughts of life, but she grew alert when a phone was placed to her ear.

The oxygen mask was removed after a full week of "comfort measures," and still she was alive but seemed to finally be in a deep sleep. My younger son, David, flew the three thousand miles to California on January 10, 2005. When she heard his voice, she woke up and called his name, thanking him for making the trip, asking about his children. Emaciated, antibiotic-resistant infections covering her, concealed cancer controlling her insides, she continued to respond with interest in others before lapsing again into quiet breathing. By the 20th, to the oncologists' astonishment, she still clung to life, although was no longer able to be roused and finally died on January 23, 2005.

Her last strong-voiced sentences had been for me. My safety. Gratitude to God for getting my husband and me through the limited visibility of fog and driving rain.

What kept her going with expectations of only a day or two left? No physicians had answers. Spunk, courage, life being a gift too good to let go of? She reminded us of that by not talking illness and just celebrating living.

Learning from the Rookie

By Diane Gonzales Bertrand

Melissa Scully became my office mate four years ago. She had finished graduate school the semester before, and unlike other new adjuncts who had shared my university office in the past, she was married, had three children, and had gone back to finish her degrees now that her children were older and more independent. She came highly recommended by her graduate professors as a person capable of teaching successfully at the college level. I welcomed her friendly personality and our common interests in literature, children, and popular culture. At the time I felt confident that I could help her with whatever problems a rookie might face in our university job situation.

In the beginning, I shared a copy of my class syllabus with Melissa. I took my job responsibilities seriously and expected the same from my students. I always followed university policies concerning absences and I stuck by deadlines for assignments. I made exceptions for special cases, but I told Melissa that I expected my students to appreciate the privilege of a college education.

Melissa followed this example, but also asked me probing questions about teaching composition and literature. As we discussed books on composition, we had a chance to share philosophies, discuss current trends, and agree that parenting often made us more humble teachers. The syllabi she developed and the results of sharing our challenges and triumphs showed me that she was genuine in her desire to be the best teacher for her students.

In her second year, however, she had a couple of new challenges in her teaching that I'd never encountered. Several international students chose to take her American literature class to fulfill their core requirement. She showed me their writing samples and wondered how to help her students succeed in her class even though English was their second language. Since I had no ESL training, I admitted that I didn't know how to help. (I even felt relieved that it wasn't my classroom problem to solve.)

I expected to see Melissa frustrated or to give way to an apathetic attitude that I've seen among college professors. Instead I saw her seek solutions. First she secured tutors for the international students at our university's learning-assistance center. Several times I overheard telephone conversations between Melissa and the director of the center. She wanted to learn better ways to help these students cope with the reading material.

In turn, the foreign students who had seen their native homeland destroyed from civil strife brought new relevance to Walt Whitman. They shared personal stories of human injustice that gave the American slave narratives a contemporary slant. American students saw their literature in ways they had never considered before, and their enthusiasm inspired and elated Melissa.

I admit that I felt envious of her excitement over the class. When those same international students came to my composition course the following semester, I was thrilled. Because of her example, I knew what to do for them to ensure their success in my classroom. I was also flattered that she would recommend my class to them.

That was also the year that Melissa had a deaf student in her freshmen composition course. Once again, I could only shrug and say, "I don't know how to help."

This time, I saw Melissa question the advisor who had placed this special-needs student in her class. She wanted to know what responsibilities the university took for accepting this student. Working with Student Services, Melissa found a counselor to work with the girl. Melissa discovered that the deaf student didn't want to wear her hearing aid because in high school she hated looking different from the other girls. Melissa was there to assure the girl that college students were more tolerant. She eased the girl's way into small group projects and discussion with the others in the class.

In the past four years, I've heard Melissa telephone students at home and tell them they had passed the absence limit and she needed to talk to them immediately. I observed other students come back to our office regularly for her personal assistance. I saw her write letters to give her students "incompletes" rather than an F in her class because she had personal information that helped her understand their circumstances.

I admired her willingness to ask "why" or "why not" rather than blindly follow university policies. She located those services that were due the students, and tracked down the students themselves rather than let their own immaturity, procrastination, stress, and depression force them into failure at college.

Perhaps Melissa was so in tune with her students' needs because her own daughter had a difficult first year in college. Perhaps she was more sensitive, more intuitive than I was. Without realizing it, I admired her gifts and found myself wanting to be more like her on the job.

Last semester I had a second-year student named Ramona who stopped coming to class without a word to me. Learning from Melissa's example, I made an effort to call the registrar, her ROTC commander, and three wrong numbers trying to reach her.

Then a week later, Ramona showed up in my classroom. "I had family problems, but I want to stay in the class."

"Why didn't you contact me sooner?" I asked impatiently. "Ramona, I called every number the registrar had. I even talked to your ROTC commander. I tried very hard to reach you."

Something in Ramona's face made me pause. I'd seen the look on several of Melissa's students when they had walked into our office and asked, "Can I talk to you alone, Professor Scully?"

Rather than stay angry, I said, "Ramona, why don't you

come to my office this afternoon? Let's talk about your absences and the work you missed."

Later Ramona told me a disturbing story about her family situation. I knew that college was the best hope for Ramona to break her family's negative cycle. She told me she was on an ROTC scholarship. If she didn't maintain her grades, she would lose it.

As I sat there listening, my eyes wandered toward Melissa's desk. I saw the university memos tacked to her bulletin board beside the pictures of her family. I could hear her voice, offering hope to her students. If this were Melissa's problem to solve, I knew that she would do everything in her power to help Ramona stay in college. She would call counseling, she would call the ROTC advisor, but most of all, she would smile at her and say, "I'll help you all I can, as long as you share this responsibility for your education."

And that's what I did.

Ramona looked happier when she left my office. She stopped by the door and turned back to say, "You know, Professor Bertrand, other professors would have said, 'So sad, too bad,' and dropped me from the course. Thanks for this second chance. I'll never forget it."

The person she really needed to thank was my office mate, Melissa. She continues to help me appreciate the reciprocal nature of teaching. Teachers learn much from their students, but they also learn well from each other. And sometimes rookie teachers even have a thing or two to teach the veterans.

A Sea of White

By Donna Amato

I looked up from my math paper when Mrs. Bauer said, "Attention class!" Normally I wouldn't have looked right away, but there was something in the manner of her voice, something that made my eyes fly to the front of the room.

"Class, we have a new student. This is Jeanine," said Mrs. Bauer in a sharp tone I'd never heard her use before.

My eyes traveled over this new person who would be joining the ranks of my fourth-grade class at St. Anthony's. I stared at her feet and worked my way up. There were black-and-white saddle oxfords, white knee-high socks, and the same navy blue, pleated skirt I'd seen a million times before. Nothing special so far. A white blouse, a little red tie, and then two enormous, brown eyes peering out at me from the darkest face I'd ever seen.

Now, Mrs. Bauer was usually very soft-spoken and kind, but she looked down her nose at Jeanine and said, "Well don't just stand there—go find a seat."

I looked around at my classmates. They all just stared as Jeanine started down the center aisle. She greeted everyone with a smile, but it wasn't returned. Where were the warm greetings I knew they were capable of, the sunny smiles I'd seen every day for the last three months?

Some of them turned their heads and looked the other way, ignoring her. She kept walking until she reached the empty desk next to mine. She looked me in the eye, as if asking my permission to sit down, the smile never leaving her face.

I looked back at her, I mean really looked at her. I could see all the uncertainty in her eyes, the pain of rejection she had seen so many times before. Still, that unwavering smile remained plastered to her face, like a shield against all the prejudice she'd seen in her short life. I smiled back at her; I couldn't do anything else. So what if hers was the only black face in a sea of white?

She sat down next to me and asked if she could borrow a pencil. Not having an extra one, I leaned over to the boy on my other side to see if he did. He turned his back on me.

I was furious! How dare he treat me that way? I wasn't one to handle anger passively. Standing up, I started toward him, but Jeanine grabbed my arm, and when I turned around, there she was smiling at me and wiggling a pencil she'd found.

There were twenty-five of us in class before Jeanine arrived. Now we had an even twenty-six, which worked out perfectly whenever we were paired up for something. No one ever wanted or picked Jeanine for a partner, so we always seemed to wind up together. I didn't mind; she was smart and we always won.

I remember the first month she was there as being very

difficult, as much for me as for her. It seemed like I was always defending her, and she was always trying to calm me down.

"How can you just sit there and smile?" I yelled. "They aren't being fair."

"It ain't a matter of fair or unfair, Donna; it's a matter of ignorance. They just don't know any better, that's all," she'd answer, her white teeth gleaming.

I often wondered if she went home and cried that first month. She certainly never did at school. In fact, she laughed most of the time. She laughed at me and my short temper, at herself, and at the hesitance of the class to accept her.

Jeanine slowly became a part of our class. Not by raging at the injustice, nor by screaming at the unfairness, but by quietly and gently making her presence known. She always knew the answers, but instead of raising her hand and bouncing in her seat until she was called on, like the rest of us did, she chose instead to wait until everyone else had a turn.

She also had a way of explaining a new concept, even when the teacher couldn't get it across to us. I think it was because she saw things differently than we did. Not always black and white, or wrong or right, but with all the various shades of gray and degrees of rightness in between.

It was her intelligence that finally won over Mrs. Bauer. She began calling on Jeanine more in discussions, and calling on her first instead of last. I guess the teacher in her couldn't overlook Jeanine's brilliant mind, but I think it was her kind and generous heart that won over the class. She was always willing to help, but she wasn't pushy. She'd simply offer her help and then wait for the kids to come to her. Slowly but surely they did, too.

By the end of the school year, Jeanine was one of us. We no longer saw her as a black person, but as just a person. Her quiet absorption into our class had changed something in all of us forever. The student had become the teacher, and we learned so much more than our textbooks could ever teach us.

I like to believe that there are twenty-five adults out there somewhere who remember the lesson taught us by a special little girl. That change doesn't come about with violence and anger, but with quiet dignity, pride in one's self, and an ever-present smile that can melt the coldest heart.

Lessons from Mr. Cain

By N. Engler

My history teacher, Mr. Cain, was a calm, mostly soft-spoken man with eyes that seemed to look right through me. I wasn't very nice to him. I was sarcastic, and one of my favorite scams was to ask him for the bathroom pass and leave class for long periods of time to visit my friends who had lunch then. I did this repeatedly and wondered why he still kept giving me the pass. I mean, he must have realized I wasn't in the bathroom, but he never said anything to me.

Then one day while I was out enjoying my free social hour, Mr. Cain appeared out of nowhere to join our little circle. I froze. Was I going to the principal's office? Mr. Cain asked me to come back to class sternly but calmly, not with anger or disgust but with a disciplined, controlled manner. I never asked for the pass again. I felt strange. A little ashamed, but mostly sad, like I'd somehow disappointed this man. And puzzled. Why was I not in trouble? Why didn't he reprimand me? I didn't understand at all.

At the end of the school year I wanted to register to become a student aide for my senior year. I thought about approaching Mr. Cain, but I was scared. I hadn't treated him with much respect. Why would he give me the position? I summoned all my courage and approached him. He said certainly he would sign the form for me and he looked forward to seeing me again next year.

That summer I ran away from home, which resulted in my being sent to live in a foster home as a ward of the state. Fortunately, my foster home was close enough to my high school so I could continue there.

Mr. Cain and my student-assistant position were there waiting for me when school began. I tried to be a little nicer to him that year, but I still had an "us versus them" attitude, especially now that my life was determined by adults I barely knew. I was defensive and built my walls ever higher and thicker to protect myself. To me, Mr. Cain was someone easily fooled, and I took advantage of his seemingly naive disposition.

One day after the students left the classroom, I remained alone with Mr. Cain. I finished my work, and as I got up to leave, Mr. Cain spoke. I can't remember his exact words, but he asked me to tell him something about myself. Caught off guard, everything spilled out of my mouth: the well-kept secret that I was a foster child, that I'd run away from home, details about my home life before I left, much more than I ever intended to say. And when I realized what I'd done, I stopped talking. No more. I had to go. I had to get out of there.

How could I have been so stupid, so vulnerable, to leave myself wide open like that? I'd given him power over me with his new knowledge, a power I never intended for him to have. Now things would be so different.

But things weren't different. Things were the same. I didn't understand. *I just didn't understand this man at all.*

Soon I faced high school graduation. I didn't know what was going to happen to me. I was going to "age out" of the foster care system in a few months and the state would no longer be legally responsible for me. My social worker was pushing for me to move back in with my biological parents. My parents didn't want me, and I didn't want them. It wasn't a promising situation. My life was in turmoil, and I was terrified. I carried this weight every day. I built the walls higher. I would be strong. I wouldn't let anyone get to me. Not if I could help it. No one would be able to hurt me.

A knock on the door one afternoon disrupted my wall-building. A delivery man with a box.

"It's for you," my foster mom said, her dark eyes filled with excitement as she handed over the long, clumsy box. "Who's it from?"

"I don't know," I said, completely baffled.

I slipped the bow off the box and carefully removed the lid. I unfolded the delicate tissue to reveal a dozen long-stem red roses surrounded by fragile baby's breath and dark foliage.

How incredibly beautiful they were! Who on earth would send me this precious gift?

I opened the card and read, "Thank you for being so nice & helpful & for being such a fine young lady. Stay as sweet as you are. —D. Cain."

To this day, I still cry when I read that card, that slightly yellowed card in its little tattered envelope. Mr. Cain, the teacher who looked beyond his rebellious student, gave me the benefit of the doubt and still held out that I was possibly a good person. Mr. Cain, the man who saw my pain and didn't beat me down with it. Mr. Cain, who saw past the sarcasm and recognized the fear, turmoil, and needs of a lost child.

And when my own children act out with words and actions meant to sear, meant to push me to my limit, build walls, and create distance, I remember . . . I remember to gather myself together, to not take it personally, and to see inside them, past the words and actions, to their real needs and respond as a kind and loving adult—just like Mr. Cain.

Student of the Month

By Terri Elders

Mr. Tower, my eighth-grade English teacher, kept an exceptionally tidy desk. No ungraded papers, no stacks of textbooks, no heaps of paper clips cluttered its pristine surface. Instead he showcased a simple matching set of rosewood desk accessories: a pencil holder, a palm-sized desk calendar holder, and twin picture frames.

One frame contained a photo of him and his wife flanking a Sears-Roebuck Santa who cradled their towheaded son. My eyes always slid right past the infant, though, to Mrs. Tower, who was also startlingly blond. Some of our moms hennaed their hair, but none were daring enough to emulate such popular platinum blonds as Carole Lombard or Lana Turner. In those 1950s days in Southern California, we tweens were all starstruck. We thought Mrs. Tower looked movie-star, drop-dead gorgeous and pondered if she got help from a bottle. But, of course, none of us would ever dare ask.

The other photo held a black-and-white Polaroid of Mr. Tower's Student of the Month. On the last school day of each month Mr. Tower brought his magical camera to school and snapped the student that he decided had made that month's most extraordinary contribution. Since he taught five classes of approximately twenty-five students each, plus sponsored Talent Club with its two dozen members, competition raged for this honor. The June choice was most prized because that student's photo remained in place through September of the new school year, impressing the next batch of eighth-graders.

Like most of the other girls, I had a crush on Mr. Tower, his neat desk, and his rosewood photo frames. All of us longed to be Student of the Month; even several of the boys admitted hoping that one day Mr. Tower would crack open the back of his Polaroid and peel away the negative to reveal a print with their likeness.

Mr. Tower never fully revealed his criteria for selection, but each month when he announced his choice, he would provide an explanation. The November student had written a highly original essay detailing why in a hundred years mystery novelist Mickey Spillane, the creator of Mike Hammer, would be just as well regarded as Edgar Allan Poe. This was just after we'd read the latter's C. Auguste Dupin short story trilogy. Mr. Tower allowed the honoree to pass around a dog-eared copy of I, the Jury, and we all gasped at the racier excerpts. But in an ensuing debate, we admitted to shivering more at Poe's The Murders in the Rue Morgue.

In February, we were not surprised when a brilliant flamenco dancer, who garnered a standing ovation at the annual talent show assembly, won the honor. Clearly, with her years of professional training, she had earned the right to the photo.

And in April a pair of fraternal twins who qualified for the statewide spelling bee shared dual honors. Some of us had grumbled just a little since the twins' parents were both English teachers, but grudgingly admitted we knew how hard the pair had worked on their memorization.

Now it was late May with only one more opportunity remaining before the close of the school year. I despaired of writing anything clever enough to equal that Spillane essay, had missed the boat with my acrobatic dance routine for the talent show, and always forgot the second "n" in mayonnaise. Nonetheless, every fourth period I would stare at the rosewood frames, straining for inspiration.

Finally, one day when the lunch bell rang, I approached the immaculate desk for a closer look at the facing photo, wondering again about Mrs. Tower's hair. I leaned down and peered closer. Could be, I thought. It's really more white than yellow.

"He's got something called Mongolism. It's a birth defect, but nobody knows yet what causes it," Mr. Tower said quietly. I looked up at him, startled. I hadn't heard him approaching. It was a second before I realized what he was talking about, and my eyes shifted back to the photo, this time really looking at the boy. So enthralled with his wife's hair, I'd never noticed that the son looked just a little different from most toddlers, with an elfin slant to his eyes.

"What's he like?" I asked. I'd heard my parents talk about "Mongolian idiots" and how they didn't live too long. I felt so sorry for Mr. Tower.

"Well, he's sweet. You can see that in the photo. Look at how he's smiling at Santa."

"How old is he?"

"David's nearly three. Just last week he took his first step, and now he's walking all around the house, even though he has to hold on to the furniture."

We both fell silent. My little brother had walked at one, so I knew that was really late to begin.

"You're the first student to ever ask about him," Mr. Tower suddenly said. "Maybe I should make you Student of the Month for that." He smiled, eyeing me speculatively.

I had to tell the truth, no matter how hard.

"Mr. Tower, I really wasn't looking at your boy. I came up for a closer look to see if your wife bleached her hair."

He threw back his head and laughed out loud. "Olga absolutely would love that," he finally said. "She's from Sweden and 100 percent a natural blond. I think I should take your photo just to repay you for your honesty."

Now it was my turn to laugh, my embarrassment quickly fading.

"I'd love it if you'd take my photo," I said. "We all adore your Polaroid camera. I'm not material for Student of the Month. But I know who is."

"Who?"

"Your son. He's learned to walk."

The following Monday, David's photo occupied the frame of honor. Before Mr. Tower provided an explanation, the classroom door opened and in came Olga and David, the boy tottering beside his mother, clutching her hand. Olga, in person, was even more glorious than her photo, her pale hair shimmering around her shoulders like an aura. She looked so much like an angel I wouldn't have been shocked if she sported a halo. Her smile lit up the room when Mr. Tower described why David was the last honoree of the year.

Just a few years later in a college biology class, I was pleased to learn that scientists had discovered that Down syndrome is a chromosomal disorder and that the derogatory term *Mongolian idiocy* had been changed.

Today I often reflect on the valuable lesson that Mr. Tower taught us. Just like the thief in Poe's *The Purloined Letter*, Mr. Tower had set everything right out front in plain sight, but in his case, nakedly undisguised. This brave teacher, in an era not noted for directness, had invited us to take notice, to be observant, to be unashamed. And to be honest. Though that photo he took of me over half a century ago has long since faded away, Mr. Tower remains in my mind as clear and sharp as black and white.

Living Life Unretouched

By Lois Greene Stone

I looked at a 1917 picture of my grandfather being sworn in as an American citizen; from the camera's angle, he appeared tall. I remember my green-eyed grandfather was a short man whose nails were stained by photographic darkroom chemicals.

On Sundays, our family drove from Flushing to Brooklyn so I could watch him photograph brides. Grandpa, in white socks, labored on his knees using straight pins to secure each fold of bridal satin to his carpet, then stood on an unpainted wooden stool to adjust veiling. He'd roll down a backdrop scene of an archway or chapel, insert a glass plate into the cumbersome tripod-mounted camera, adjust the bride's head tilt, then squeeze a rubber ball to seize that moment. His slender fingers removed each thin dressmaker's pin before he'd put his shoes on and roll up the backdrop.

In a small room illuminated only by reddish glowing light, I was fascinated with magic images that appeared from blank paper.

"Teach me, teach me," I begged. Grandpa placed my tiny

hands around a hard, circular metal gadget that clamped a photo above a mirror.

"What should I do if I smush one and the thing breaks, Grandpa?"

"Save your hand-framed picture, but just throw away broken mirror glass. That you've made something is important."

He smoothed my limp flaxen strands with fingers that smelled of his familiar tobacco and chemicals, and praised my efforts. He allowed me to open his bulky, brass cash register with its big round numbers, hear its bell signal open, remove a nickel for a treat.

In the cafeteria below his studio, I bought a nickel charlotte russe (sliver of white cake in circular cardboard topped with whipped cream and a crimson cherry) to share as we'd shared mirror picture making.

Some Sundays I didn't see Grandpa. Later I learned that his "away" days meant touring with the United States presidents; he photographed every one from Taft through Truman.

"Grandpa," I asked one Sunday morning in October 1945, "can I pretend to be a bride and hold your fake flowers? Can I?" He kissed the top of my hair as I was still shorter than he was, then said, "Just a few minutes till the first bride."

"But I want to hold the bouquet."

"Here. Don't grab or clutch. Place your left arm underneath, then drape, not drop, your right hand over the handle. Just the back curve of your hand should gracefully appear."

Fake calla lilies were not as light as they looked and their cascade too big for my tiny frame. I felt pretty, embarrassed, awkward, and wonderful all at the same time. It was the ending of every fairy tale I'd ever read.

Grandpa grinned. "Don't grow up too fast, monkey. Just enjoy being young." He adjusted the fake bouquet, which in black-and-white film looked magnificent, but in real life looked helpless and dull. "Ready? Now turn." He put a piece of veiling over my face.

"When I'm grown, will you buy me my very own wedding gown?"

He smiled softly; the corner of one eye seemed to be collecting fluid. He pretended to take my picture, and I giggled.

His first appointment came toward me, her lace train pulling along the rug. Her headpiece was tall and crisp; my pretend veil now looked like a wrinkled hankie.

Grandpa labored with lighting, forcing it to make faces glow or the folds in satin gowns shimmer. But this bride was wearing all lace, which didn't reflect light, so he made every detail sharp as snowflakes against a windowpane. Like weighty fake flowers that looked light and lovely, he strained with every detail so pictures would seem natural.

After that sitting (I never knew why it was called a sitting when brides were always standing), Grandpa gave me a penny to buy Indian nuts we'd share. "Always feel you're important," he said cracking shells, dropping crumbs into a metal wastebasket and passing nuts to me. "Whatever you do, feel, or think is special."

My eyes used to smart when I left the red-lit darkroom place and reentered the incandescent lighting of his studio. He was working; I was enchanted.

He developed a technique (using my mother posing in one of her fluffy hats) for photographing a person in front of multiple mirrors without flashbulb reflection. He made a postage-size stamp of one image for pasting on World War II overseas mail that didn't have to pass through censors as V-mail. I glued four tiny images of my mother on the blank area of a broken picture mirror.

Grandpa seemed to do everything: taking cash, moving huge lights, photographing, developing, dusting a counter. I absorbed this message of self-esteem and dignity in labor; of making tasks seem as light as pictures of fake flowers when I knew that they, in real life, were heavy and clumsy; that one could love work.

Grandpa taught me, by observation, that nothing is menial. Whether one photographs a president on gelatin silver, a bride, or a Sunday-best, dressed-up child, each is equally important. On his knees sticking silver pins into fabric and then wool carpet, or onstage with Eleanor Roosevelt during a speech, he still had dignity.

He helped me develop pride in completing a task, allowing myself satisfaction, and I knew from the word "refugee" that he had pursued, not compromised, his dreams. He had courage to accept "no" along with "yes," and this made him "tall" no matter that the yardstick measured only 5'4".

Grandpa acknowledged when he lacked dexterity or ability. At a table filled with sable brushes of various sizes, a retoucher removed a face blemish. "Retouching fools the eye," said Grandpa, "but what we really are before sable wipes out imperfection is never fooled." My aqua eyes looked at this giant who knew everything there was to know about everything, even when I didn't really understand what he meant.

I watched photos being oil-colored with transparent paint. When I pushed cotton in quick, circular strokes over my own children's black-and-white photographs decades later, I realized that some simple creative things do last and remind us of our ability to produce with our fingers, eyes, and imagination. And a "worker's" task of hand coloring, then cleaning up messy cotton-ball clumps stained with pigment, wasn't menial. How that lesson runs through my life! Grandpa said that I should sometimes *see* the way I'd like things to be, not what is really there.

I recently investigated more about some of his political photographs when the International Museum of Photography decided to start an archive on William Metz, photographer. But he was Grandpa, who tickled my back, taught me to enjoy creating with courage, to accept rejection, and personally prove that all labor has significance.

I last saw him in 1956 when he was ill and frail. I was on my way into the adventure of marriage and he to the retirement of Miami. But, like his photos in original folders in the International Museum of Photography, he was still tall and strong and "unretouched."

Watching for the Rebound

By Terri Elders

I try to do the right thing at the right time. They may just be little things, but usually they make the difference between winning and losing.

—Kareem Abdul-Jabbar

"It's not Wimbledon," Kelly warned, "so you have to watch the players, not just the ball." I nodded knowingly. Thanks to his patience, I now could recognize a full-court press.

I'd grown up in southwest Los Angeles, refereed for John Muir Junior High Girls' League, and watched neighborhood kids play H-O-R-S-E at Harvard Playground on sizzling summer afternoons. As a schoolteacher at Jordan High in North Long Beach in the early sixties, I'd always volunteered to chaperone on basketball nights. But until now I knew next to nothing about how the pros set up plays.

Kelly, a former star point guard for his state championship–winning high school team in St. Louis, Missouri, had also played for the navy and coached in a number of venues. In his view, basketball was a metaphor for life. Both were filled with obstacles, challenges, and sometimes defeat; both offered opportunities for progress and sometimes victory.

It was Sunday, April 20, 1986, Long Beach, California. We were ensconced in a booth at Panama Joe's in Belmont Shore, munching quesadillas, watching Michael Jordan nearly single-handedly play the Celtics. It was Jordan's first season with the Bulls, but per Kelly, Michael was a one-man show. Kelly had taken me to brunch in an effort to ease my anxieties about my acceptance of a new job that I wasn't certain suited me.

"Stop worrying. Stay in the now," he said. "It's like basketball. The winners never give up. They can be twenty down and come from behind. You can't predict the final score, let alone guess what's going to happen in the next play."

Jordan and the Celtics battled magnificently, but I had a seminar to attend, so at the half we headed for my condo. "I'll be back in about three hours," I said, reluctantly turning from the televised excitement. "Leave me a note about who wins."

When I returned, I found a scrap of Kelly's trademark yellow legal-pad paper by the phone. "Jordan scored again, but McHale grabbed the rebound and . . . you'll find the next play on Plant-it Earth." I scurried to the crimson lacquer vase where I kept my weekly bouquet from the local florist. There amid the peppermint carnations, I found the next yellow slip.

By the time I'd collected all the clues on this merry treasure hunt, running from my stuffed Paddington Bear in the bedroom, to the kitchen microwave, to the medicine cabinet, I was laughing aloud. Though saddened to learn that after his herculean sixty-three points, Jordan's Bulls ultimately suffered a first-round loss to the Celtics in double overtime, I ended that day happier in mood, less fearful of the future.

Fast forward: Tuesday, January 27, 1987, Inglewood, California. We were ensconced in row 12 of the senate seats at the Great Western Forum, surrounded by 16,000 wildly cheering fans. I turned to Kelly just as the cheerleaders streamed onto the court. "Explain to me once more why the fast break works so well for the Lakers."

"Well, it's the ultimate offensive weapon," he began, passing me some peanuts. "No matter how much Portland's going to try to slow them down, keep your eye on how fast the Lakers get the ball down the court. Watch how they really sprint after a steal or a rebound."

Just before New Year's my long-ill mother had succumbed from complications related to Alzheimer's. To distract me from my despondency, Kelly had shelled out $165 per seat, which, he remarked, weren't even padded.

"Grief's a part of life," he told me. "But you have to move on. It's not always about the layups, the successful scoring, but also the rebound." Kelly glanced at me. I nodded, getting the message.

"I'll take you down to where they exit at the end of the game so that you can get a sense of just how big these guys are," Kelly promised, settling back to watch the game.

"Here's your starting lineup," the announcer roared, and Kareem Abdul-Jabbar, Magic Johnson, James Worthy, and the others bounded onto the floor. I took a deep breath, and let showtime absorb my attention. Though a bit afraid of Clyde Drexler and Kiki Vandeweghe, I loved the way Magic Johnson fed the ball to "The Captain," Jabbar, at the post. At the close, we stood near the Laker's exit, and I'm convinced that Magic winked down at me.

Saturday, December 26, 1987, Glendale, California. We were ensconced on the sofa of a tiny furnished apartment where we were recovering from injuries sustained in an attack by muggers in Belize after our swearing-in ceremony for the U.S. Peace Corps. Kelly awaited reconstructive surgery on his forehead, wearing a navy watch cap to cover a gash in his forehead. I'd undergone bypass surgery in my left arm, where the brachial artery had been severed. I needed extensive physical therapy to regain range of motion in that arm.

I'd been preoccupied all Christmas Day and worried about rejoining our Peace Corps group in the spring. "Let's go to the playground," Kelly suggested. "Nobody will be there the morning after Christmas, and we'll play H-O-R-S-E."

Though he'd tried tirelessly, he'd failed to teach me to make a layup. But this morning to encourage me to move my arm around, he taught me the granny shot, an underhanded loop that he said had been made famous by Rick Barry, one of the greatest free-throw shooters of all time. This time I actually sank some baskets. "It's all about the physics," he explained. "You compensate for your lack of height with this shot."

So we horsed around at the playground and then strolled

back to the apartment, breathing in the chilly winter air. "You're learning more about the game," Kelly said.

"And life?" I asked. He chuckled.

Later we watched the Lakers take on the Utah Jazz in an away game that had me nervous. The Lakers coach, Pat Riley, had promised a repeat on their '86–'87 championship season, but the Jazz were formidable rivals.

"It's going to be fast break versus pick-and-roll," I told Kelly confidently. "But Stockton and Malone aren't going to win this one." I was right. The Lakers won 117 to 109.

Kelly and I recovered from our injuries and rejoined the Peace Corps group in March. In June the Lakers won the NBA playoffs. Belize City fans drove their pickups through the streets that sweltering night after the final victory, honking and hollering, nearly as noisy as the fans at the Forum.

The next morning I found my Lakers T-shirt had been stolen from the clothesline outside my house on Regent Street. I spied it on a Rasta later that afternoon. Win some, lose some, I shrugged, grinning to myself and thinking of Kelly.

In mid-August, 2008, nearly two dozen of Kelly's relatives and friends sat in a circle on a balmy afternoon in St. Louis, Missouri. He had died suddenly, but not unexpectedly. We flew in from California, Washington, Tennessee, and Virginia to comfort one another through the pangs of bereavement.

Though it might not feel right quite yet, I, myself still grieving, await the chance to rebound. "You have to move on," my life coach always told me. "You can't predict the final score."

The Hat That Looked Like a Rug

By Delores Liesner

Iburst into tears after the first sentence I heard from Marv Hegle—"Why are you wearing a rug on your head?"

I raced to the car, reasoning through tears that there was no way he could have known what an oppressive and abusive atmosphere I'd been raised in—where nothing I said or did was "good enough." Even with this knowledge, it was difficult to resist the memory of old taunts returning with this perceived insult.

His wife rushed after us, the newcomers they'd just met at a large metropolitan church, apologizing. "Don't take his comments seriously," she urged. "It's just his weird sense of humor." And then she invited us to their home. I wasn't sure I wanted to subject myself to more "weird humor" but felt obligated, and, surprisingly, found out it was exactly what I needed.

Marv had an amazing effect on me. But at first I was wary. I heard laughter emanating from his home when we approached the front door, and I self-consciously wondered if he was again joking about my crocheted hat. I'd left it in the car, and was glad I did because I saw him glance at my bare head and then turn with twinkling eyes toward his mate to receive an obvious message. "My wife thinks I may have hurt your feelings by commenting that your hat looked like a rug," he began. All eyes turned toward me, and my mind raced for an appropriate response.

He laughed and added, "I'm sorry, but it really *did* look like a rug to me."

I stared at this short, balding man we'd just met, then at his wife, her eyes twinkling as she let out an exaggerated sighed, "Marrrrv," and shook her head hopelessly. His young son simultaneously moaned, "Daaaaad," and I suddenly realized they'd apparently experienced this situation many, many times before. Instead of feeling hurt, I suddenly felt challenged to one-up him, and my husband gasped as I retorted, in kind, that Marv was perhaps subconsciously longing for a "rug" to cover his almost-bald pate. I followed up with an offer to crochet him one. Marv laughed uproariously in approval, and the rest of the afternoon was spent in lighthearted banter.

Our friendship grew as Marv mentored us in our faith-walk—challenging me, especially, that I could continue to choose to allow life's offenses to wound me, or I could deflect them with humor and grace. I'd never known I had a choice.

He toughened me up weekly, saying things like, "Never try to teach a pig to sing—it wastes your time and annoys the pig." My childhood-trained insecurity questioned whether he'd heard me sing and meant it personally. But I soon saw his message wasn't personal and quickly learned to enjoy his simple humor instead of analyzing potential hidden meanings in every joke. He taught me to laugh at myself after my first attempt at baking French bread resulted in hollow, hard loaves; he offered to buy a hundred and donate them to the local police station as billy clubs.

He allowed me to laugh at him, too, and to discover that his humor was a hard-fought victory over many physical and personal trials. Marv didn't come by this knowledge without pain.

Needles, surgeries, and medications were evidence of the diabetes that would eventually take my mentor, but to Marv they were more opportunities to share his faith by being a living example. I never left his home without feeling uplifted— by his attitude, a devotional he shared, or the lesson behind a silly joke that would remind me of the hope that still remained in my life.

The baggage I'd stored from years of childhood abuse was no longer an overwhelming burden, but an opportunity for growth and encouragement to others. The message I internalized as a child—that if a person failed they were a permanent failure—was now replaced with the realization that I was not only human but didn't have to allow the past to come between me and another person. My relationships grew astoundingly once I realized that forgiveness was a choice to love—and was something others also wanted from me.

An extremely rare disease caused Marv's two middle sons to be born blind—and though he and his wife wept, those feelings of pain were rechanneled as Marv set about teaching his boys that same emotional freedom he was teaching me. Pity wasn't going to suffocate their possibilities—or mine. So life was hard. If you looked beyond the hairstyle, the clothes, and the home—outward wrappings, as Marv put it—you would see that everyone had burdens.

Today, those two successfully employed young men are happily married and a joyful reminder of a legacy I was privileged to have as part of my life, too. Instead of thinking "if only," I began to trade places with people I observed and wondered what mysterious thing they imagined me to have that they might long for. I was surprised to identify the things my mentor had verbally affirmed—a writing skill, compassion for the wounded, a good memory, a sense of drama, and an inclination to defend against injustice. I was astonished to find myself auditioning for and receiving small parts in local theater and having articles and stories accepted for publication. Like forgiveness, courage had also been his gift to me.

Courage was also a choice for Marv as his disease controlled more and more of his life and hospital visits became frequent. I still crocheted, and scraps of every color yarn filled a bag I carried on the way to each hospital visit. Those visits resulted in several unique hats that he wore like a crown, even though they all still looked like rugs to him.

He proudly told me he even wore them to work and then invited me to his classroom. He'd changed his career to teaching at a vocational school for the blind. The classroom had no windows and was dark. There was no reason to turn the lights on except for sighted visitors. Marv introduced me as the friend who made his wonderful hats, and I felt more love in that dark classroom than I'd felt in any I'd attended as a student. I knew these students "saw" much of what I'd missed most of my life.

Marv wasn't a perfect man and often reminded others that God didn't use us because we are good, but because *He* is. Because of that self-effacement, I trusted Marv. He knew more about my imperfections than I wished he did, but loved me anyway. He didn't point out my imperfections or faulty motives or petty unkindnesses. Rather, he exposed only the positive results of the choices he taught me to make.

Marv taught that living on purpose is a choice. I soon discovered that dying on purpose is also a choice. One of the last things he asked me to do was feed him chocolate, joking that it could be his "kiss of death." That may sound macabre to some, but he knew I understood him by now and could hear the love behind his choice of words.

Thanks to Marvin Hegle, I choose to rise to my full five-foot height and find humor and hope in every life event so that others might also experience the forgiveness, love, and courage that began with Marv—and a hat that looked like a rug.

A Teacher's
Caring Heart

The Little Things

By Mimi Greenwood Knight

Considering this was my third go-round with the whole starting-school business, you'd think the first day for my son, Hewson, would have been a snap. Not so. My shy, little fellow had spent kindergarten at a tiny preschool where there were only a dozen kids in his class, less than a hundred in the whole school, and I was teaching four-year-olds not fifty feet from his classroom door.

This was a big school. This was for real. He'd be there for seven hours and I'd be an entire twenty minutes away from him. His two big sisters were at the same school but in a building clear across campus. It took all of the self-control I had to feign delight at this wonderful new adventure he'd be embarking on, when all the while I was knotted up inside.

To make matters worse, there was a complication switching him from our little private school to the public school system. A last piece of paperwork didn't come through in time so Hewson actually started school one day behind the other kids. It wasn't bad enough that they'd all probably been together in kindergarten, even pre-K, but he was starting on the second day of school. He might as well have a sign on his forehead declaring "New Kid."

I'd been furtively scoping out the first-grade teacher over the past year, but the jury was still out on what I thought of her. I tried to tell myself that just because she wasn't a big smiler didn't mean she wasn't warm and loving with the kids. It would have been easier, though, if she'd smiled when I left my tiny guy at the classroom door—for my sake, if not for his.

I knew that a quick good-bye would be easiest on Hewson, so I forced myself to make a dash, then couldn't seem to get much farther than the hallway. The school bell had rung so the hall was empty for now. This particular part of the school was an older section that actually still had keyholes. A glance both ways, and I eased down on one knee to catch a peek at Hewson just to assure myself he'd be fine. I hoped the teacher wouldn't look over and notice a big eye watching her.

I twisted my head around to rotate my inch-and-a-half view until I found Hewson. He was sitting at his desk clutching his backpack, his eyes fixed on the teacher's every move. He looked so small. I thought about flinging the door open, snatching my boy, and running for my life. Homeschooling might be an option.

I checked the hall again. I was still alone, so I got comfortable on both knees. If anybody caught me, I hoped it would be another mom who'd understand why a grown woman was kneeling in the hall with her forehead against the doorknob.

As I surveyed the scene in the classroom, I realized what was going on. The day before, Mrs. Tosso had obviously sent each child home with an identical blue folder full of papers for their parents to read, sign, and return. Of course, Hewson didn't have such a folder. I watched him get more and more anxious as his teacher went from child to child collecting blue folders. The closer she got to him, the more frantically he tore through his backpack, hoping it would somehow appear in there.

That's it, I thought. *I'll just open the door and explain to my child that his mother messed up. I should have started him here last year. I shouldn't have dropped the ball on the paperwork so he could have started with the other kids yesterday. I don't know why I was ever trusted with children.*

Hewson kept one eye on Mrs. Tosso as she worked her way toward him, still desperately rifling through his backpack for that all-important blue folder. My hand was on the doorknob when she reached Hewson's desk. *She'll just have to write me off as "one of those moms." I can't take this any longer. I'm going in to save my baby.*

That's when I watched her squat down until she was eye-to-eye with Hewson. She said something I couldn't hear, and I saw Hewson's body visibly relax. She slipped over to her desk, retrieved a blue folder, and handed it to Hewson with a reassuring smile. I dropped back on my fanny right there in the hall and cried.

Why does this have to be so hard? More important, what

had I done to deserve God blessing my child with this warm, understanding teacher? In that one small gesture I knew everything was going to be okay. And it was. Mrs. Tosso taught Hewson to read and write and add. She helped him fall in love with chapter books and to give and take with other kids. She informed him that he's a good writer. She taught him about butterflies, the sinking of the *Titanic*, how to grow a bean plant, and where our state is located on the map. But most important, she cared and taught me to let go and trust someone else to have my child's best interest at heart.

Katherine Hadley said, "The decision to have a child is to accept that your heart will forever walk about outside of your body." Ain't it the truth? I thank God for teachers like Suzie Tosso who He put down here to make that voyage a little bit easier.

Buck Tyler's Example Taught Best

By Mickey Burriss

W e moved to Allendale, South Carolina, and a new house just a few days before I began the tenth grade in 1952. Previously a tourist stop on Highway 301 between Florida and Maine, Allendale began booming then as a residential community for families of workers constructing the Savannah River Plant, referred to as "the bomb plant."

I fell in love with the town because hunting and farmlands lay just a half mile past the city limits and only a narrow broom straw field lay between our house and the school's back door. On opening day, I crossed the field to the front entrance and signed up for classes. The sudden influx of construction families doubled student enrollment, which added fun and excitement to the town and school.

Being a city boy who yearned to live in the country, I signed up for agriculture class. This allowed me to join Future Farmers of America and placed me in Mr. Buck Tyler's classroom. His was not a tenth-grade curriculum but a cross-section of about ten rawboned boys from ninth to twelfth grades. All reared in Allendale, some had taken "ag" for several years. Farming, which had only been my dream, was their life.

Mr. Tyler's first order of business was for students to choose a project for the year. I believe the others expected this because as Mr. Tyler called each name, the students described projects ranging from raising a shoat, fattening a calf, growing sweet potatoes, raising winter wheat, erecting a prefabricated metal corncrib, to—"I don't know."

Buck Tyler's blue eyes stared dead into mine. "Why don't you know?"

I pointed out the window. He could clearly see my home across the field, sitting on the corner of a dirt side road and the paved street to Swallow Savannah Cemetery. "I live over there and don't have room for a project."

He walked to the window and peered out, turned, and said, "I'll think about it."

I left school that day thinking I had slid by again. I say *again* because we'd moved around a lot following construction projects, and I'd learned how to avoid work and responsibility by cultivating pity—a new and ignorant lad in town. After school the next day I spotted Mr. Tyler coming through the broom straw, his red hair glistening in the autumn sun. Over his shoulder he carried a grub hoe, an ax, and a shovel. I met him on the back steps. He leaned the tools against the house and said, "You can plant centipede."

I'd never heard the word "centipede" (a type of grass), and

I stood there studying the ends of the tools propped menac-
ingly nearby.

"Come on, I'll show you." He walked around to the front
yard. I trudged behind. We stopped at the corner where the
two roads met. He waved his arm horizontally in a semicir-
cle, like he was blessing the plumb thicket and said, "Dig
these up. Let me know when you finish." As he headed back
toward the school, he stopped and said, "Take care of my
tools."

"Yes sir," I yelled over the broom straw and glanced again
at the dreaded instruments already ruining my afternoon.

At school several days later, Mr. Tyler loaded the nine of us
into a school bus and drove to a farm. We walked through a
pasture accompanied by the farmer who explained to Mr. Tyler,
"I found her when I noticed what looked like a buzzard fight.
The calf's hind portion was hanging out. Had to have been
dead several days 'cause they were trying to get at it. "

When we reached the cow, I was relieved there was nothing hanging. Mr. Tyler removed his shirt. The cow stood with
drooped head slung low, not even swishing her tail to ward off
the fly swarms. I think she was too sick to swish. Mr. Tyler
rammed his arm clear to his shoulder, out of sight, up the cow's
birth canal and began dragging out hunks of dead calf. I almost
upchucked from the smell alone, and I stood fifteen feet away.
I wondered how he tolerated the odor and sight of the rotten
calf so cheerfully. He joked, "Any of you boys want to get some
hands-in-training? Give you an A." A farm boy volunteered,

but Mr. Tyler said, "Just kidding. Better not. You could get hurt, but you get an A for trying."

After the cow was empty, he shoved a garden hose about five feet in her and flushed her with disinfectant. He washed with soap and water and poured some chemical on his arm.

During the ride back, I pondered what Mr. Tyler had just performed. It made an everlasting impression. He didn't have to help the farmer or the cow. He taught school, not veterinary medicine, but forty miles from Augusta he was Allendale County's closest thing to a vet. Mr. Tyler was a helpful man, and I believe he felt sorry for the farmer, and we all felt sorry for the cow. In that hour he showed us, indelibly, without mentioning a word, the importance of taking good care of your animals and helping your neighbor. Mr. Tyler provided a strong, positive example for us boys, and we affectionately called him Mr. Buck. He later told the class the cow recovered.

It took me thirty days of chopping and grubbing before I dragged the last plumb bush into the field next door. Mr. Tyler returned carrying a ball of masonry twine and a burlap sackful of grass. He told me to wet the bag every day and store it in the shade. This was easy.

We walked to the front yard, and he knelt down at the corner of our lot, tied one end of the twine to a sixteen-penny nail, and stuck the nail in the ground. He stretched the cord to the opposite property boundary and anchored the line with another nail. He looked up at me and said, "Get the ax."

I lit out around the house and ran back with it. He chopped

several holes about a foot apart along the string line, pulled some sprigs of centipede from the sack, placed them in the chopped holes, and stepped on them, mashing the dirt around the sprigs so only the tip protruded from the earth. He handed me the ax and said, "Plant the sprigs about this far apart," and held his hands out to indicate the distance. "When you reach the end, move the string twelve inches. Repeat the spacing until the yard is completely sprigged. If you need more grass, let me know. I want to inspect when you finish."

I did as he said for a day or two, but my ax-chops grew farther apart and the string moved wider and wider with every relocation. When he inspected, just before Thanksgiving, he marked about fifty places with his heel where sprigs were too far apart. As he left, he said, "Good job. In a year or two your yard will have a thick carpet of centipede."

I guess he was right. We moved when school closed for summer, but thirty years later I rode by, and it looked just as he'd predicted. I've never forgotten Mr. Buck and how he taught me about meeting responsibilities and diligently doing any job. I also never forgot that milk cow is spelled "milch" cow.

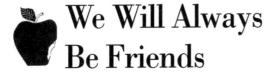

We Will Always Be Friends

By Miriam Hill

"Oh! Too bad you have Tyler in your second-grade class this year," remarks the first-grade teacher as she scans my list of students. "He won't do a thing for you. Last year I had to retain him."

The first day of school I approach the sad-looking boy with dirty blond hair slumped at a desk labeled with his name.

"Hi Tyler, welcome to my class," I say as he looks at the floor and doesn't respond. When I help him during the day I notice he doesn't finish his work and his writing is messy. He attempts some lessons, but as soon as he puts his answers on paper, he erases what he wrote, leaving long, black eraser lines that seem to underscore his failures.

I learn that Tyler's grandmother, Carolyn, works in the school cafeteria and is raising him and his older brother. "His parents have problems," she confides during our parent-teacher conference. "I thank the Lord Tyler got you for a teacher. He never liked his teacher before, and he adores you."

A few months later Carolyn shares surprising news.

"The boys and I are leaving Florida and moving to Tennessee.

Tyler's older brother is friendly with the wrong crowd. Maybe moving away will help."

When I say good-bye to Tyler, I assure him, "We will always be friends." He nods and lets me hug him.

Years later, I respond to a knock on the door and discover a tall teenager balancing on a skateboard. "Remember me . . . Tyler?" he inquires, and suddenly I remember that struggling student in my second-grade class. He says he's traveled here to see his father . . . and me.

After that Tyler begins visiting me when he's in town each summer, and we talk about his life, the importance of making good choices, and the reasons I'm proud of him. He graduates from high school, starts his own tree-trimming business, and moves into his own apartment.

During a recent visit he's excited to show me his new red truck. Afterward we sit on the deck, munch on homemade chocolate chip cookies, and talk. Tyler brings tears to my eyes with his words.

"You know, I didn't have a good family, and I'm lucky my grandmother and you have influenced my life. I'm grateful God gave you to me."

As this successful young man drives away in his new truck, he waves from the open window and yells, "Hey, Mrs. Hill, you were right. We will *always* be friends."

To Touch a Child

By Nancy Julien Kopp

"**I**t's a man!" "We've got a man!" "Our teacher's a man!"

My classmates' comments echoed down the hallway, getting louder and more frequent the closer I got to my fifth-grade classroom. My heart beat a little faster as I peered cautiously into the room.

Sure enough—there he was—the first male teacher at Lincoln School in the southwest corner of Oak Park, Illinois. The year was 1949, and Lyle Biddinger beckoned me with a welcoming smile into his first class. He served in the navy during World War II and finished college on the GI bill after being discharged. We would be the springboard for his teaching career.

All twenty-one of us in that room knew that something big was happening here. Men taught in high schools and colleges. Women took charge of the grade school classrooms. Yet, here he was—a man; not only a man, but a good-looking one whose smile could melt the hardest heart.

Mr. Bid, as we soon called him, taught us in both fifth and sixth grade, and what a teacher! Because of him, I hurried through breakfast every morning and raced out the door, in a hurry to get to school, eager to see what new adventure he had planned for us. He related stories about his service in the navy, taught us games, and made us laugh. Other teachers walked around the playground at recess time watching students play. Not Mr. Biddinger—he played *with* us. Kids from other classes joined us in those playground activities with this special man. They envied us when it was time to go in, because we had him for the rest of the day. We were proud as peacocks, too, for he was ours. Each of the twenty-one students in that class claimed him, hung on his every word, and loved him.

The main topic of dinner conversations at twenty-one homes centered on what Mr. Biddinger had done that day. What Mr. Biddinger said. What new game Mr. Biddinger taught us. It wasn't too many months into that first year when parents began to complain. "He plays games all day." "He doesn't teach them anything." "What are they learning?"

I don't know what Mr. Biddinger or the principal said to appease these uneasy parents, but life in the fifth grade did not change. We continued to play games, but we learned a great deal too. Every game we played reinforced the facts and figures in our textbooks. Those games were educational tools unheard of in the 1940s. School wasn't meant to be fun. It should be hard work, dull, and boring. Or so our parents thought.

At Christmastime, the room mother collected money from

each student's family, then talked to Mr. Biddinger's wife to come up with the perfect gift for him. Our excitement knew no bounds when we presented him with a hunting jacket at the class Christmas party. The gift truly surprised him, almost overwhelming him with emotion. That was the best part of Christmas for all of us that year. It was the year many of us discovered that giving really is better than receiving.

Fifth grade flew by. The lazy days of summer drifted by, and we returned to Lincoln School in September, eager to see what Mr. Bid had in store for us in sixth grade. That year proved to be as good as the previous one. We were still envied by the students in the other sixth grade, and we continued to preen our feathers whenever we had an audience.

We learned new things daily, adding to the long list of facts and figures Mr. Biddinger taught us. I probably remember more of what I learned in those two grades than at any other time in my grade school years. Only a very good teacher could have accomplished that feat. After becoming a teacher myself, I realized the quality of Mr. Bid's teaching. I knew then the gifts he gave on a daily basis. He helped us develop values and ethics as well as knowledge. He showed us that hard work and fun can line up side by side. He listened to whatever questions we posed or something we needed to discuss.

We moved on to junior high after tearful farewells to our special teacher. Two years later, Mr. Biddinger attended our eighth-grade graduation. We had been his first class, and I like to think that we were just a bit more special than any other to him, as he was to us. All the girls marched down the aisle of the gym that day, wearing high heels for the first time. After the ceremony, Mr. Bid told me that I walked better than anyone else in those new shoes. For all I know, he gave the same compliment to every one of the girls. Nevertheless, it made me feel special on my graduation day, the same way I had felt every day of the two years I claimed him as my teacher.

Now I would like nothing better than to take him to lunch one day. I would reach across the table, take his hand in mine, and tell him how much he meant to all of us. Yes, he was our first male teacher and certainly the best. He armed us with knowledge and instilled self-confidence in our own abilities. But most of all, he reached out and touched all twenty-one of us with everlasting love.

Bonnie's Song

By Pam Bostwick

"I sang it fifty times, and I never get it right," I complained to my singing teacher, Bonnie.

I was learning the song "America the Beautiful." My hearing loss made it difficult for me to follow the alto harmony. Because of my partial sight, I had to use a magnifying glass to read the words.

"Come on, sweetheart! Try singing the line again. I know you can do it," Bonnie squeezed my hand. "I'm glad to remind you of the words until you memorize them."

Her encouragement gave me the confidence I needed.

I squared my shoulders. "I want to work hard to sing good like you."

It took hours of going over the song, but Bonnie's patience and my persistence to keep going paid off. I finally sang it on my own. Bonnie grabbed me and danced around the room, exclaiming, "You did it."

I grinned. "You're the best teacher ever." I paused. "I did do a good job, didn't I?"

"You sure did!" She hugged me. "I'm proud of you." Bonnie valued and accepted me. I learned many songs after that because she believed in me.

Then one day she broke the news to me, "I'm sorry, Pam. I have to move."

My stomach lurched with that sinking feeling. I cried a long time in her arms.

The last time I saw Bonnie, we shared a special lunch and chatted and laughed quietly. We both dreaded that time of parting.

Finally, Bonnie walked out on the porch with her arm around me. My mom drove up and waited in the car while Bonnie and I clung to each other. I fought to keep from weeping as she whispered, "You've been like the daughter I never had." She'd been that mom for me too, yet I couldn't tell her. The lump in my throat was so big. Bonnie kissed my cheek. "I'll miss you."

The horn blared behind me. For a fleeting moment, I wondered if Mom wished we were close like Bonnie and I had been. I couldn't remember the last time my mom had kissed me. Bonnie lifted my face to hers. "I don't like good-byes. You'll forever be in my heart. Always think of me when you hear our favorite song."

I nodded my head as we spontaneously broke into "Oh, beautiful for spacious skies."

Our voices flowed together, and I wondered, *Why in this free country don't I have a choice about my friend leaving me?*

I dragged my feet to the car and slowly climbed in. Tears blurred my eyes. Even if I could have seen enough to look back at Bonnie, I didn't because it hurt too much.

While we sat in the car, Mom said, "You're a big girl now. You can be tough about this. She's just a music teacher. We can find another one."

I bit back a retort because Mom didn't understand.

The memory of Bonnie's voice made me feel warm all over again. Mom wasn't going to take that joy away from me. I took a deep breath and said carefully, "I appreciate you wanting to find another teacher for me, but nobody can replace my friend Bonnie."

"Bonnie's an old lady like me. How can she be your friend?"

I wondered again whether Mom wanted to be closer. But relating to her was like building a bridge across the Grand Canyon. How could I do the impossible?

Then as I remembered Bonnie's embrace, I saw the way to build that bridge. "Mom, can I give you a hug?"

She hesitated, then replied, "Well, sure, I guess." It was a tentative hug on both our parts, but it was a start.

Bonnie never gave up on me, so I wouldn't give up on my mom. This new challenge of trying to get along with her would help me not miss Bonnie as much.

It's amazing that only seven months with Bonnie, at age eleven, still impacts my life as an adult. Bonnie's devotion and our song will live on in me. To this day, I can't always sing on key, but, thanks to Bonnie, I sing even if my efforts are a "joyful noise." She filled up an empty place in my heart. Now I'm free to give my children and grandchildren an outpouring of tenderness.

Each Fourth of July, when "America the Beautiful" is sung, I feel Bonnie near, her rich, glorious voice singing the high notes. On earth, Bonnie sang like the birds. Now she sings with the angels in heaven.

Camp Ozanam

By John J. Lesjack

Too soon old, too late smart.

—Confucius

Summer of 1950, Carsonville, Michigan.

A counselor at Camp Ozanam, the summer I was thirteen, seemed to take a special interest in me. He watched from the bench as my cabin won the softball championship. He stood and cheered as my cabin won the track championship. He applauded as we won the talent show. I thought, at first, that my counselor supported my cabin because he liked winners, but I was wrong. . . .

My counselor's attention seemed totally innocent at the time, but because of negative publicity given the Catholic Church and some of its priests in recent years, my memories of camp had begun to be tainted with dark feelings when I decided to do some digging and write my camp story. I felt I'd lived with suspicion long enough. It was time to enlighten myself about the real motivations of Mr. Loren O'Dey.

I loved camp. I had people to play sports with, which I liked because I lived far from other families. Hikes in the woods allowed me to breathe in the scent of evergreen trees for the first time. Where I lived, we had open fields full of weeds. I got to sleep in a cabin and eat three times a day without anyone complaining about food prep or cost. Plus, we had leather-craft lessons during the day and campfire stories and songs at night. My only disappointment was that I never found any fireflies— something I'd never seen. But even that was okay. I didn't want camp to end.

A thin, frail, balding man of twenty-three, Loren sat with me in the mess hall, visited my cabin, and watched from the beach while I went swimming in the cold water of Lake Huron with my group. He waited for me after church, and we walked around the grounds together. Why was he showing me so much attention? I wondered. Had I done something wrong?

That fall, Loren often called my house and left messages with my mother. He invited me to dinner at the home of his parents. He left his phone number, so I could call him. He sent me a birthday card. He just assumed, or so it seemed, that we were friends. When he did get me on the phone at home, he asked how I was doing in school (terribly), at home (terribly), with friends and other people (terribly), and in sports (great). I never once asked how he was doing.

The time he visited my house, I gave him a bone-crushing handshake. I'm embarrassed about that now, but I'd been on the football team, lifting weights, growing stronger, and I wanted him to notice my physical strength. He was ten years older than I was. I didn't know about his health at the time, and I didn't mean to hurt him.

What puzzled me over the years was why he had tried for so long to be my friend. He just appeared in camp one day and hung on all during my high school years and well after I went into the navy. But the most mysterious thing about him was that he never asked anything of me.

While researching Camp Ozanam for this article, I learned a truth or two that filled in some blanks. The camp, located on the eastern coast of Michigan, was financed in 1950, as it is today, by the St. Vincent de Paul Society. Children who were/are underprivileged and suffering familial hardship were provided an opportunity to enjoy a summer camp environment.

I didn't know my father's death six months before camp caused me to be labeled "underprivileged." There I was having the time of my life, not realizing that I and my fellow campers had suffered "familial economic hardships." The truth is I'd have loved Camp Ozanam anyway, even if I'd known. The only mysterious part was Loren O'Dey hanging around like my shadow. What was his story?

Turns out, the St. Vincent de Paul Society hired students from Sacred Heart Seminary to work as camp counselors. Loren O'Dey, a seminarian studying to be a priest, became one of those counselors. He was practicing a philosophy unique to the St. Vincent de Paul Society where members use their own resources, such as the telephone and the mail services, and they share their possessions, like dinner at the home of their parents. He was also practicing the group's specialty: the gift of his presence. Loren O'Dey stuck by me, trying to get me to grow spiritually at a time when I had suffered the loss of my father. Loren recognized my neediness and tried to help me by offering person-to-person service in the tradition of the Blessed Frederic Ozanam, a French scholar, and the patron saint Vincent de Paul.

Loren never became a priest. He left the seminary, due to his poor health, and went home to live with his parents. His health rallied a bit while he was working in downtown Detroit, where he also met a woman he wanted to marry. He proposed, she accepted, but he got sick again. He sent this information to me in a letter while I was in the South Pacific in the navy. I never heard from him again.

My mother later wrote that Loren had passed away.

All the years he contacted me, I didn't know what he wanted, and neither did anyone else. Now that I understand, I'm not resentful that he felt sorry for me and reached out. The poor, the underprivileged, the needy, those of us who've never seen a firefly—we are appreciative. Even if it takes some of us fifty-seven years.

Gentle blessings, counselor, wherever you are. Your efforts were not wasted.

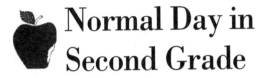

Normal Day in Second Grade

By Linda Kaullen Perkins

Up until that moment, my day in second grade had been calm—only one case of head lice, one upchuck, and two fights on the playground. No fire drills, no broken bones, and no angry parents. I felt lucky.

"Okay class," I said. "You'll have fifteen minutes to clean your desks. I'll set the timer for the first five. Start by throwing away your clutter. Ready . . . Set . . . Go!"

The noise level went up about ten decibels. Everything ran smoothly for three minutes. Then Todd ran up to me, his brown eyes snapping. "Danny's cryin'. Gots somethin' screwed in his tongue."

"What?" I said, feeling my luck slip a little.

Todd shook his head, setting his wild curls springing. "Won't take his head out of his desk. Come on."

I yanked Danny's desk lid higher and leaned over him. "What's wrong?" I whispered.

A freckled nose and watery, blue eyes appeared above the raised desk lid. "Thith thin ith in my ton."

I rushed around to the other side of his desk for a better view of Danny's tongue and stood shocked, watching the metal coil from a spiral notebook swinging back and forth. Never had I witnessed such a sight. I knew I had to do something—and fast!

"Hold still, Danny," I ordered, grabbing his tongue. The timer beeped wildly and Melinda Jane yelled, "I'll get it."

"I'm classroom monitor today," Howie shouted.

"Reset the timer please, Howie," I said, glancing up. "Boys and girls, you have ten minutes to finish." Who was I kidding? No one was going to miss this sideshow. The class watched like a flock of owls at a mouse parade.

I gave the wire a gentle twist. The tongue squirmed worse than a slug being salted. I refrained from yelling, "Yuck."

"Ah, ah, ah." Danny's eyes widened and his face paled. He was in pain.

"Ooh, I'm sorry, Danny. I must have turned it the wrong way." I let go of his tongue and tried to keep smiling. It was obvious that the righty-tighty-lefty-loosy law didn't apply to notebook wires and tongues. I took a deep breath. "Everyone go back to your seats."

By now Danny had clamped his mouth shut and burrowed his head deeper into the open desk.

"Pleeease, Danny. I think I can get it this time," I lied.

Fortunately for me, Danny was a meek boy. He eased open his mouth, terror shining in his eyes. My fingers wrestled with the slippery spiral, and it finally twisted free.

"Here it is," I said, holding up the trophy wire. Applause broke out as relief swept through me.

The principal, who happened to be walking down the hall, stuck his head inside the classroom. My stomach tightened. How long had my boss been listening to the circus taking place in my classroom?

"Mr. Vogel," Todd shouted, "Mrs. Perkins unscrewed Danny's tongue."

The principal looked in my direction and a broad grin broke out across his face. "So that's how you keep your classroom under control."

A Real Somebody

By Donna Hedger

W hen I look back over my childhood school years,
there are few memories that stand out in my mind.
The only thing I remember about first grade, for instance, is
the left- and right-hand chart on the wall, a girl who wanted
to be friends that I thought was a boy, and that we had to spell
"supercalafragalisticxbaladocious" for extra credit. (Obviously
I still can't spell it) Second grade I was chosen to help bring the
milk cartons to the lunchroom; third grade, another girl and I
drew horse pictures, and our classmates were impressed with
our artistic abilities; fourth grade I have few memories of except
a vague sketch of the teacher's and students' faces. And then
there was fifth grade.

It was probably the loneliest year I've ever had. Because of
a home life that was unstable, I didn't fit in. I was a nervous,
ADHD-type child who was socially inept. When I tried to sit
with the other kids at recess, they turned to me and told me
that they didn't want me there. It was definitely a time when
there was not a lot of love and affirmation in my life. As a

result, I became withdrawn, sullen, and moody.

But there was one bright spot in fifth grade: Mr. Brody. I don't remember too much about his class. Only that we had a mock courtroom trial in which I was chosen to be a lawyer. I don't remember his teaching style, any books we read, or outstanding lessons we covered. The main thing I remember about Mr. Brody is that he made me feel loved. He made a dejected child feel like she mattered in the world. When no one else saw value in me, he did. I remember one time I was absent for two weeks because of issues at home. When I returned to school, he didn't lecture me about how much work I needed to make up, but simply greeted me with his big smile, gave me a hug, and told me how happy he was that I was back.

My favorite memory is Field Day. We were having different kinds of competitions, and I was the last runner on my team in the relay race. I was ahead, and I ran with all my might (in my mind, it plays out in slow motion, like in the movies!). I can still see Mr. Brody at the finish line, jumping up and down, cheering me on. How symbolic of the significance a teacher's role can play in our lives. To cheer us on in life's journey. To make us feel like we are a real "somebody." I won the race, and Mr. Brody lifted me up in the air and spun me around, sharing in the joy of my victory. That moment stands out in my childhood, because it was such an unusual feeling for me to be a winner at anything. And no matter how turbulent times were at home, no matter how the other kids shunned me, Mr. Brody made me feel like I was a winner in life.

I still get tears in my eyes when I think of Mr. Brody. I'm sure he has no idea how his simple acts of love, encouragement, and kindness made a difference to a child who really needed it. Perhaps some teachers think it's the amount of knowledge they impart that's the most significant aspect of their jobs. That is definitely a main goal. But equally important is the ability to make children feel loved. Thanks to all the Mr. Brodys who do just that.

She Taught Me So Much More than Math

By Michael Segal

Mrs. Pillar was one of my second-grade teachers. She taught me math, and, at that time, I assumed it was everything I would need to know about the subject. However, I'll always remain indebted to her for her additional "math lessons" more than a decade later.

As a sophomore in college, I was involved in a near-fatal "accident" when I walked into the middle of a robbery at a convenience store. One of the thieves shot me in the head—"pumping a bullet into my brain." The thieves, as well as most everyone else, thought that I was dead or would soon be. Obviously, they were wrong. However, it was a severe and difficult battle getting back into the mainstream of life. I had to drop out of college to be hospitalized. Even after I was discharged from the hospital, I endured many hours of intensive therapy. I had to relearn practically everything, including walking, talking, and yes, even math.

To help me with that task, Mrs. Pillar volunteered to come to the hospital and later to my house once a week to work with me. At first, the material she presented was very basic math. Then, as time progressed and I made progress, my "homework" became progressively more difficult. I remember very vividly how she would come to my home on Sundays, sit with me at the kitchen table, and throw various coins on the table. She would ask me to show her thirty-eight cents, seventeen cents, sixty-three cents. It was challenging, but she also made it fun. After a year and a half, I'd progressed sufficiently, both physically and mentally, to return to college. Once there, I continued therapy regularly, but at least I was back at the University of Texas.

Four years later I graduated at the top of my class and went on to graduate school. As the years went by, I always kept in touch with Mrs. Pillar. However, one day my parents informed me that Mrs. Pillar had been hospitalized because she'd suffered a stroke after undergoing open-heart surgery. Now it was my turn to help her.

When I walked into the ICU at the hospital, Mrs. Pillar was in a hospital bed and could not speak. I was struck by the irony of it all. Nothing had changed, except for who was in the bed and who was standing beside it. I promised Mrs. Pillar that I would be back and that I'd work with her just as she'd worked with me years earlier.

As the days went by, I saw Mrs. Pillar progress each time I visited. One day, I pulled some coins out of my pocket, dropped them on her bed, and asked her to show me twelve cents. The nurse thought my action was extremely strange until Mrs. Pillar smiled briefly. I began working with her just as she had worked with me years before. I'd name an amount, and she would put the dimes and pennies together to equal that amount.

Mrs. Pillar was eventually transferred from the ICU to a private room and then to a rehab room. As she moved from room to room, there was no doubt in my mind that she was improving. When I visited, I'd always ask her to tell me something good. At first, her family members jumped in and said, "Mama's doing so well," or "My sister is doing great." However, I'd quickly raise my hand and say, "Mrs. Pillar, you tell me something good." Slowly and hesitantly, she'd answer my question, and as the days went by her responses became quicker and more fluent.

Mrs. Pillar made wonderful progress and was eventually discharged. One day I called her to wish her a happy New Year. She spoke into the phone quite fluently and said, "Happy New Year to you and your family, Michael. Thank you for everything you've done for me."

I quickly remarked, "And thank you for everything you've done for me." Mrs. Pillar was one of my second-grade teachers, but she taught me so much more about life than mere mathematics.

A Greater Kind of Love

By Linda Mehus-Barber

Although it was his first year of school, Michael had already been thrown out of two schools. He came to us near the end of his grade-one year, defiant and ready to prove to everyone that no one could tell him what to do.

His teacher plopped down on the staff room sofa. "That Michael's a waste of space," she spat.

I rolled my eyes, tired of her complaining, "Come on, Louise, he can't be that bad."

"Are you kidding me? This kid's a prime example of why they should make abortion retroactive. He doesn't have a chance—no dad, and his mother's a loser."

The bell rang and I stood up to leave, thankful for an end to this ugly conversation. Three steps before I hit the doorway, I heard her snarl behind me. "Well, he'll be yours in three months. Good luck!"

I shivered as I made my escape. *Some people don't belong in the classroom,* I thought.

September came. Michael was on my class list, and I

wondered if he would show up. With the fresh anticipation that September always brings, I collected my supplies and headed to class. I always looked forward to greeting a new group of students, but this year the specter of those staff room warnings cast a shadow of unease over my enthusiasm.

With my arms full, I started down the hallway. A whirling dervish came from nowhere, forcing me to sashay aside. It was Michael. He bulldozed his way past the other children, sending two unsuspecting seven-year-olds smashing against the wall.

"Yeah! Teacher's here!" he yelled to the others. "Let's go!"

He flung open the classroom door and quickly became leader of the pack. Darting up and down the rows, he skidded to a stop whenever he found a desk he thought he liked. He'd peer inside, then wiggle onto the seat to see if it fit. He eventually chose one at the back of the fourth row, near my desk.

An hour into the day, Michael decided to entertain the class by sitting in the garbage can. Chuckling, he pranced over and plunked into it bottom first, folding up like a "V," his scrawny legs sticking out at a forty-five-degree angle. The rest of the children giggled. My instinct was to ignore such obvious attention-seeking behavior, but I couldn't. Michael was stuck.

An overwhelming desire to spout my first mini-lecture of the year came over me. "Michael," I began, but instead I bit my tongue and strode over, somehow managing to remain calm and control the seething frustration bubbling inside. I steadied the can between my feet and thrust one arm under his legs, the other under his armpits. I yanked, and the can broke free. As

I stumbled backward, my heel slipped on the freshly waxed linoleum, and my legs shot out from under me. In a scene that would win top prize in *America's Funniest Home Videos*, the two of us lay sprawled in a heap on the floor. The class erupted.

Later, in the middle of the math lesson, Michael popped out of his desk, stretched out in the aisle, and began a set of sit-ups. *Lord, I'm going to need patience for this one*, I thought.

That night, I knelt in my living room and prayed more fervently than usual. *Dear God, I'm not going to make it through this year without your help. Let me see Michael through your eyes.* In the silent, meditative moments that followed, I wondered yet again why I had become a teacher.

I taught at a tough school where the staff turnover was high—only the strongest stayed. Some moved on to schools where the children were easier to teach, while others simply crashed and ended up on long-term disability. With Michael in my class, the year was more challenging than usual, and the days dragged by. I was constantly vigilant for even the slightest sign of positive behavior to reinforce. The reward was simple—often a gentle smile and a touch on his shoulder, or a moment of eye contact with a wink, and sometimes a hug. Gradually, Michael began to blend in with the rest of the children, although to keep him on track he needed attention about every thirty seconds. I was exhausted and Christmas holidays were a welcome relief from the daily drain on my energy and emotions. I deserved this vacation.

One bitterly cold day after the break, I took up my supervision post in the dark, predawn hours. The grounds were eerily empty. I trudged through the snow toward the southwest corner of the schoolyard, glad I was wearing heavy work socks under my mukluks, a down-filled parka, and woolen mittens. As I gazed across the frozen playground, I saw the silhouetted shape of a small child stumbling through knee-deep snow, fighting the icy blast of the north wind as it threatened to suck the breath out of his little body. Snow crystals, like shards of broken glass, whipped across the treeless field, and for a moment, the hazy form all but disappeared. Even in the semidarkness, I recognized the figure. His hands were shoved into the pockets of his tattered jacket. He hunched forward, his hood pulled up to provide at least a little protection from the deathly cold, its fake fur trim framing his tiny face. It was Michael. *Why do kids like this never stay home from school?* I sighed.

As he drew closer, he recognized me. His little legs churned faster and he beetled toward me. He flung his arms around my waist, causing me to step back to catch my balance. A pale face peered up. His nose was running and tears welled up in his red, swollen eyes. He was shivering uncontrollably and through chattering teeth, he groaned, "I'm so sick!"

My head dropped, and I looked down at him. "Then why didn't you stay home?" I asked, knowing a selfish motive lurked behind the question.

"I couldn't," he sniffed. His little arms reached around further, tightening his embrace. He snuggled closer and continued, "I had to come to school—to get a hug."

I found my arms involuntarily wrap around him, pulling

him firmly against my body. My chin rested on the top of his hooded head. A tear escaped and instantly froze to my cheek, and on that bitterly cold morning, an unexpected burst of love entered my heart—a greater kind of love—God's love for this little boy. In that moment, I knew why I was a teacher.

I've often thought about Michael. I don't know what happened to him after he left our school, but I do know that my understanding of love changed because of him. Over the years, other children like Michael appeared at my classroom door, and I took what I'd learned about love and gave each of them a reason to get out of bed and come to school. Daily I would pray, *Dear God, let me see these children through Your eyes.* The answer to that desperate plea softened my heart so that I was able to love even the most unlovable.

I taught for ten years at that school. During my last year, a tough and hardened little girl came to me with the label "behavior disordered," a label she'd earned by biting, kicking, and scratching her previous teachers. In June, as I was packing to move on, a tearful Jamie crept silently to my side and shoved a crumpled, ragged-edged piece of paper into my hand. I smiled, then carefully unfolded it and smoothed out the wrinkles. "Why do you have to go?" she had scrawled. "I'll miss you. Thank you for teaching me to love."

I knelt down. My arms reached out, then wrapped around her shoulders and pulled her close. My chin rested on top of her matted curls. That greater kind of love had touched another heart.

Must-Know
Info

MUST-KNOW INFO

The CORE of Teaching

Dr. Jeffrey Zoul, author of
Improving Your School One Week at a Time

Today's K-12 teachers are faced with what—at times—seems like an insurmountable number of programs, initiatives, daily tasks, and responsibilities. During those times when it seems as if there are simply not enough hours in the day to keep up with all that must be done, successful teachers remember that at its essence, teaching is a people profession requiring highly refined people skills. As educators, we must remember that programs are subordinate in importance to the people charged with carrying them out. In order to succeed, teachers must be able to rely on core values to carry them through a school year and—hopefully—a long and rewarding career in education. Although such core values will logically vary from teacher to teacher, our very best teachers are highly proficient in the CORE of teaching: Communication, Observation, Relationships, and Expectations.

Although individual style is important and educational values among teachers can be unique, I discovered early in my career that there are four key factors that all successful teachers emphasize. I identified and wrote about these at length in *The 4 CORE Factors for School Success*, which I coauthored with Dr. Todd (Whitaker & Zoul, 2008). These four essential teaching responsibilities, represented by the acronym CORE, are essential to teacher success. Whether one is teaching kindergarten in an urban area or high school geometry in a rural area, to succeed, one must act in purposeful ways that emphasize these four simple, yet powerful, teaching principles. Listed below is a brief summary statement related to each of these four essential teaching responsibilities vital to success in the most noble profession of all: teaching.

Communication—The importance of communication in any profession cannot be overstated, yet this is particularly true for educators. Teachers must communicate effectively not only with the students they teach, but also with parents, colleagues, administrators, and community leaders. There are virtually hundreds of methods teachers employ to communicate with these and other school stakeholders during the course of a school year. Although technological advances have changed many of the ways in which we communicate, great teachers still find time to call parents of the students they teach to make a personal connection and strengthen the home-school bond. When calling parents, teachers focused on the CORE follow these five general guidelines:

1. *Call Early.* Do not wait until a problem occurs to make

that first phone call home. Call parents early in the year to set the stage for a successful year of teaching and learning together.

2. *Call Often.* Get in the habit of making at least two phone calls to parents each week, with at least one of these being a call home about positive student performance.

3. *Be Honest.* Parents appreciate when teachers are honest with them about their children. Teachers must be direct in communicating news about undesirable student behavior or academic performance while delivering this honest assessment in a dignified, respectful manner.

4. *Find the Good.* Great teachers find something positive to communicate even when calling about concerns they have in other areas.

5. *Listen.* This is the most overlooked aspect of effective communication in teaching. Great teachers make it a point to actively listen to parents when they are talking about their child so that, together, they can strive for improved student performance.

Observation—Teachers focused on the CORE must be careful observers of all that occurs within their classroom on a daily basis. They must also observe student performance over time, monitoring progress and adjusting their teaching accordingly. Although teachers spend the majority of their day observing students in their own class, it is important to periodically consider another type of observation: peer observation. Even our most effective teachers struggle in some area or at some point in time during the course of a school year. Although teaching can be an isolated profession, one way great teachers break that mold and find new ideas for improving their own performance is by observing a colleague at their school in action. What better way to find ideas for succeeding in the classroom than observing a teacher who has faced similar obstacles and overcome them? Find time at least once each month to observe another teacher at your school teaching a lesson. In turn, invite a colleague into your own classroom to observe you in action and provide feedback. Great teachers are always willing to learn new methods for improving their practice and are equally willing to share what they do best by inviting others to observe and learn from them.

Relationships—Teachers focused on the CORE realize that the relationships they build and maintain with their students are a key factor in determining how much these students will learn and how well these students will behave. If the three most important words in real estate are "location, location, location," the parallel for teachers is, "relationships, relationships, relationships." Teachers must cultivate and maintain relationships with students, parents, teachers, and administrators that are built on trust and mutual respect. Great teachers find ways throughout the year to go the extra mile to create a positive relationship with each student.

Expectations—The importance of expectations is closely tied to that of relationships. Teachers focused on the CORE establish crystal clear expectations for their students on the very first day of school and spend the next 179 days of the school year building relationships with students so that they will want to meet those expectations. Alas, setting clear and lofty expectations for student learning and student behavior is not a one-day proposition. Teachers must enforce these expectations daily in a consistent, firm, and fair manner. It is not unusual to see students who misbehave in one classroom behave perfectly in another. In such cases, the variable is not the students, but the teacher, and the difference between the two teachers is likely related to the expectations they have for students and the way they go about enforcing them. Teachers focused on the CORE follow these three principles related to expectations:

1. *Establish and Communicate Expectations.* Effective teachers do this at the very outset of the school year, taking pains to communicate precisely what will occur throughout the year in terms of teaching, learning, and behavior. These expectations are few in number and focused on the *major*, as opposed to a lengthy list of rules focused on the *minor.*

2. *Consistently Clarify, Reiterate, and Reinforce Expectations.* Great teachers realize that simply having and stating expectations at the beginning of the year is not enough. They find systematic ways to regularly promote and reinforce these expectations.

3. *Serve as a Model.* Successful teachers model effective atti-

tudes and practices in the area of expectations, setting high expectations for themselves and acting in ways consistent with the classroom and school expectations.

Having strong core principles guiding their daily actions and behaving in strategic ways designed to fulfill the CORE values of Communication, Observation, Relationships, and Expectations are the hallmarks of great teachers. Even during times of inevitable changes in education, great teachers remain focused on these essential human relations skills. Teaching is a profoundly important profession because all teachers make an impact on the students they teach; those focused on the CORE are certain to make this impact one that is positive and lasting.

MUST-KNOW INFO

MUST-KNOW INFO

Responding to a Crisis

Lisa Bundrick, LMSW,
NYS Certified School Social Worker

Crisis situations can be experienced by individuals or by groups and can occur in the home, community, work place, or at school. A crisis is a stressful event, unique to each person, that is above "normal" life experiences, such as child abuse, suicide attempt, car accident, or divorce. After experiencing a crisis an individual may have a variety of feelings including numbness, helplessness, fear, confusion, or anger—there are no right or wrong feelings. How one responds to a crisis situation varies, depending on the person's perception of the crisis. However, there are some general tips that can be useful when responding to individuals in crisis. First and foremost, under no circumstances should a suicidal or homicidal student be left alone. Depending on the crisis situation, additional steps and strategies may need to be employed.

Provide a Safe Environment: Converse with the student privately and provide him with your undivided attention.

Offer Support: When someone is in crisis the most important thing that can be done is to offer support to him and reassure him that you are unconditionally there for him.

Be Calm: A student's behavior may mirror yours. Be understanding and supportive, but try not to express your feelings about what the student is telling you. If the student senses a negative reaction from you, she may stop talking.

Talk Less and Listen More: When someone is in crisis, we often want to help by talking. This is not what should be done in a crisis—this is a situation of "less is more." We have two ears and one mouth for a reason. Sometimes, it's not what you say, but what you *don't* say. Listen carefully to the person in crisis and offer your support. Allow the student to speak at her own pace, and watch her body language for subtle cues that you may be talking too much. Silence is okay.

Think About Nonverbal Communication: Literally get down to the student's eye level and look him in the eyes. Nod as he talks. Position your body toward the student, not away from him. Be genuine and caring.

Acknowledge Feelings: Each person will have a different reaction to a crisis. Let the student know you hear that she is angry, scared, frustrated, and so on. Don't try to minimize the student's problem by saying: "I know how you feel," "Things will get better," or "You are making a big deal out of nothing." You don't know how the student feels, things could get worse for her, and as her problem, it is a big deal to her! It's better to say: "I can't imagine how you feel right now."

Offer Reassurance: Let the student know you will be there for him. Stay with the student until he is calm and/or until help arrives. Ask him what he needs and what you can do to help.

Don't Make Promises That You Can't Keep: Some crisis situations in a school setting may involve child abuse disclosures or disclosures of suicidal feelings or attempts. A student may approach you by saying: "If I tell you something, you have to promise never to tell anyone. . . ." Don't promise confidentiality. You can, however, promise to offer your unconditional support, help, and privacy by reporting your concerns to only those who need to be aware in order to best help the student.

Seek Support: Let the student know what steps you are going to take to help her. Let her know who you are going to contact and why. If possible, have her make a choice about the support people she feels can best help. These choices might include a social worker vs. counselor, or mom vs. dad.

Follow Up: When you see the student again assure him that you are still there for him and care about him. By smiling and saying "hello" when you see the student, you let him know you care.

In a crisis situation, it is important for educators to consult with their school crisis intervention teams and follow their school policies. By exploring additional readings and training to become proficient in this complex topic, educators will be better equipped to help a student who is experiencing a crisis.

Writing Letters of Recommendation

Jennie Withers, author of Hey, Get a Job! A Teen Guide for Getting and Keeping a Job

Jessica was a student anyone would love to teach, coach, or employ. I knew her well from both class and afterschool activities, so when she asked me to write a letter of recommendation for her, I answered quickly and easily, "Absolutely!"

After Jessica left I sat at my desk, paralyzed with fear. I wanted to write a compelling, effective letter of recommendation for Jessica, but I didn't know how. I was only in my second year of teaching, so I did what any novice teacher should do: I asked a veteran educator for help. Her first question was, "Do you want to do it?" It hadn't occurred to me I had a choice. Like many teachers, I believed if a student asked, I was obligated to write a recommendation letter.

First Things First: How do you feel about this student? You don't have to say yes, and can do more harm than good if your heart's not in it. Be sure you can write a very positive letter.

When deciding whether or not to write a recommendation,

trust your instincts. Has the student made enough of an impression on you that you can honestly write a glowing recommendation? Has she been a discipline problem? Even if you decline, you can still be supportive by gently explaining your reasons and helping her to find someone more suitable. Remember, this is not a time to lecture a student about misbehaviors; it's a time to help her move in a different direction.

The Student Must Help You: No one will think much of a letter that says, "I really like Jessica. She's a cool kid." Here are some things you need from the student:

- **Resume**—It will tell you about her accomplishments and activities. If she doesn't have one, there are many resources like Microsoft Word and resume websites like www.teens4hire. org to guide her through creating a resume.

- **Audience and purpose**—Where is this letter going and what is its purpose? You need a clear understanding of why the student wants to attend this college, apply for this scholarship, or get this job so you can word your letter accordingly. And, you need to know where to send it.

- **Reminiscences**—Students ask you to write a letter because they believe they did positive things in your class. Brainstorm with them to get a complete list from their perspective.

- **Time**—Students must give you a deadline, but they also must provide time for you to create. While I try to be flexible if the student wasn't given much time for the application process, I don't write letters for the last minute, fly-by askers. The reason I give: "I don't have time to write a letter that does you justice."

Getting Started: The letter should open with the name of the student you're writing for, the extent of your relationship and the length of time you've been acquainted, and the reason the student is applying. The opening paragraph should also set the tone. Like a thesis statement, it introduces the reason you chose to write the letter.

To Whom It May Concern:

I am pleased to write to you on behalf of Jessica Johnson, who is applying for admission to Best University. I have known Jessica for two years. She was a player on my JV basketball team, and is now in my Senior English class. Jessica is a gifted student and athlete, but perhaps more important, she is an outstanding citizen.

Prove It: This is the portion of the letter where you have to show—not tell—the reader that the student is as great as you think she is. Vague praise or neutrality is avoided with examples and anecdotes. Your goal is to illustrate one or more of the following:

- scholarship
- citizenship
- leadership
- community and school service
- unusual circumstances—something about the student's life that makes her extraordinary

Jessica has been an honor student as well as an athlete through-out her high school career. For most students, this is a difficult bal-ance, but for Jessica, it wasn't challenging enough. She became a volunteer at our local nursing home during her sophomore year. This year, during a unit on oral history, she came to my English class with an idea. She wanted to implement a program called "adopt a grandparent" which pairs a student with a resident at a nursing home.

Jessica's peers respect her immensely, so it was no surprise that my class enthusiastically jumped on board. Jessica spearheaded this enormous undertaking. She said it was important to her because the elderly had interesting histories that we needed to hear and learn from. It is because of Jessica's insight that every resident in the nurs-ing home has a regular visitor.

Wrap It Up: In conclusion, summarize why you are recom-mending the student, and remember, there is a difference between *recommend* and *highly recommend*. The selection com-mittee will likely pick up on this subtlety in your letter, so state it plainly and honestly.

I'm sure you will read of Jessica's grades, sports abilities, and of her accolades and awards. There are many examples such as the one in this letter that demonstrate her impeccable character. Jessica displays intelligence and leadership abilities that are well beyond her seventeen years. I highly recommend Jessica for entrance into Best University. She is a student who will be an invaluable asset to your institution. If you have further questions, please don't hesitate to contact me.

Sincerely,

Jennie Withers, West High School

What's Left?: Your letter is typed in business format and is no more than one page in length. It will reflect poorly on the student if there are errors, typos, grammar mistakes, or your letter is unclear, so have someone else proofread it and then do another draft. Be sure to show your final draft to the student and verify that it is what she needs.

After the final polish, print and mail the original, keeping a copy for your own files. If she needs a recommendation for another purpose, the original can be tweaked, and can also be useful as a model for future recommendation requests.

Document the date you sent the letter, as this will provide proof that it was sent. If you hand it to the student, make a note of the date and time. If you e-mail it, you have the proof in your "sent documents" folder. If you are using regular mail, send it in a verifiable form such as certified or registered mail, or at least use a return receipt. After all your hard work, it would be heartbreaking to discover that your letter never arrived and the student was disqualified.

The last thing I strongly suggest is to pat yourself on the back. It is an honor to be asked to write a letter of recommendation. It means you are a respected teacher and you have a good rapport with students. Your letter might be the deciding factor in a student's future!

MUST-KNOW INFO

Tips for Struggling Readers

Liana Heitin, MA Ed,
Cross-Categorical Special Education

Astudent who struggles with reading skills is a student who may be less than successful in other academic subjects. Here is some basic information that can help you to assess and remediate the problem for many students:

A student who misreads a word is doing one of three things:
- Seeing the wrong letters
- Saying the wrong sounds
- Guessing

A teacher can differentiate between the first two types of mistakes with a quick and easy test at the time of the misread:

1. Cover the misidentified word with your hand.
2. Repeat the mistake and ask the student what letters he saw in that word. For instance, if the word was "fleet" and the student read "feet," you would say, "You said the word 'feet'. What letters did you see in "feet'?"

3. If the student answers F-E-E-T, then he likely saw the wrong letters as he was reading. If he answers F-L-E-E-T, then he saw the right letters but is making incorrect letter-sound correspondences.

The third mistake profile—guessing—is the easiest to identify. Students who are guessing most often get the first sound or two correct and substitute a known word that begins with the same sounds. Often the length of the word or an unusual letter combination seems intimidating, so the student glosses over the remaining sounds. Here are some examples of misreads that are the result of guessing:

Student reads:	Actual word
want	water
play	placed
before	beside
strong	strange
weekend	western

Now that you have identified the problem, you can begin to remediate it.

For students who are seeing the wrong letters:
These students, classically labeled as dyslexic or learning disabled, will require instruction through repetition. Their mistakes will include reversing, transposing, skipping, deleting, and adding letters or sounds. It is imperative that these students practice and memorize common orthographic patterns,

including all digraph sounds, blends, and affixes. Other important strategies for these students include:

Emphasize the importance of what words look like. While most emerging readers pick up patterns in words and recognize spellings that mimic each other (e.g., *feature* is like *creature* with an *f* instead of *cr*), students with this type of reading disability will not easily make these connections. The teacher should point them out to get the student thinking about orthographic patterns.

One-on-one guided reading instruction. Once students have memorized common patterns, this strategy works well. Each time the student miscues, the teacher should immediately address the mistake by hiding the misread word, repeating the student's mistake, and asking the student to recall the letters. After correcting the mistake, ask the student to re-read the entire sentence for comprehension. Consistently calling attention to the miscues will force the student to see every letter in a word rather than glossing over difficult sounds. This method helps strengthen the student's visual imagery, or ability to make mental images of words. Adept readers can envision words, remember the number of letters in a word, and manipulate letters to form new words, but struggling readers need direct instruction to develop these skills.

For students who see the correct letters but form sounds that do not correspond:

- **Rule out a deficit in phonics.** Does this student know all the letter/sound correspondences?

- **Make flashcards of letters and digraph sounds and test the student.** If the sounds are known, the student may be struggling with an even more basic reading skill: phonemic awareness, or oral sound differentiation.
- **Challenge the student to break oral words into individual sounds.** Ask the student to break a few words into their sounds (e.g., stripe=s-t-r-î-p).

Often, both phonemic awareness and phonics are in place, yet there is still a disconnect between what these students are thinking and what comes out of their mouths. Train the student to hear this incongruity by pointing out miscues. Again, a quick and easy test can come in handy. In this case, the critical component of the test is repeating the student's utterance. Hearing someone else repeat the mistake helps students catch the incorrect letter/sound correspondence. When doing this with new students, I repeat the mistake slowly, drawing out each sound to give them a chance to compare the sounds and letters. (You said *fffeeeeetttt*. What letters do you see in *fffeeeeetttt?* What comes after the *f?* The student will soon realize the *l* sound has been deleted.) Eventually, students strengthen the connection between what they're seeing and what they're saying. They will start to catch their own mistakes, hearing incorrect sounds as they leave the mouth.

For students who are guessing:
Guessing is often the result of impulsive behavior. Chronic

guessers are typically students with attention problems and hyperactivity who want to rush through their work. They will need frequent reminders to take their time. While many teachers provide incentives for finishing work on the clock, these students may need incentives to slow down. As a student tires of reading and begins to lose focus, guessing becomes more and more frequent. I often know it is time for a break when a student guesses several times in a row. The student has likely entered an inattentive zone—perhaps an intrusive thought or environmental change has caused the distraction—and the trance must be broken. Even a one-minute stretch break, a game of tic-tac-toe, or a stroll around the room can be surprisingly refreshing, and just the thing to get the student to stop guessing and start reading.

Students with an aptitude for sight words, or high frequency words that are memorized, make up another group of guessers. These students may seem like fluent readers because they rarely stumble as they read. Yet when they come across a new word, they are forced to guess because they rely on their word memory, not phonics. For them, I advise supporting their strongest skill. Let them practice the word by sight until they have it memorized.

MUST-KNOW INFO

Getting the Most from
Your Substitute Teacher

D.C. Hall, Board Certified Substitute Teacher

My day starts at 7:30 AM. Or 8 AM. Or maybe 8:30 AM. Every day is different. I check in with Debra. Or Donna. Or maybe Loretta. Every day is different. Then I teach math. Or music. Or maybe English. Every day is different.

I am your substitute teacher.

More often than not, I have no idea what my day will be like when I leave home in the morning. On some days I walk down the street and teach history to pampered eighth graders. On other days, I drive forty-five minutes and teach fourth grade-level reading to high school students in jail (oh, they call it an "Intensive Halfway House," but it's a jail, plain and simple). My best days are when I return to a familiar classroom to fill in for teachers who know me and trust me. Those are the days I actually get to teach.

Teaching as a profession offers personal fulfillment, and substitute teaching offers many of the same rewards. But, at times, substitute teaching is a thankless job. School systems are designed to keep outsiders out and, like it or not, subs are outsiders. Additionally, many "real" teachers are wary of subs, and have little confidence in any substitute's teaching skills. Finally, many students see subs as untrained teachers waiting to be toyed with.

A teacher *can* make substitutes an effective and vital part of the teaching arsenal. Here are some ways to do that:

Expect success, not failure. Give the sub a chance to get it right. Leave the current lesson plans. Worst-case scenario— you'll have to reteach the lesson. But, you were going to have to teach it anyway when you left that busy work, weren't you? Take the chance. Best-case scenario—your students are up-to-date, and you'll have an extra day for fun stuff.

Most schools require teachers to have "sub plans" on file for unexpected absences. Some teachers have up-to-date files designed to keep their students on pace with the semester's plan, but most teachers have "special" plans for subs—plans that consist of "make work" or worse yet, material that was previously covered. And anyone who has ever tried to convince a bunch of hormonal, hyperactive thirteen-year-olds that they need to stay focused on the same useless, nonsensical worksheets that they already completed three days ago will attest to just how much fun that can be.

Decide for yourself—observe the sub. When a neighboring teacher is out for a day or more, take the opportunity to "scout" the substitute(s). There's no better way to judge how a substitute handles a class than by watching him or her in action.

Do you want someone "like you" to fill in when you're out? Guess what? That's very common. Most of the teachers who request me over and over do so because my personality and teaching methods are very similar to theirs.

Measure the sub by your student's results. Leave work. Real work. The work you would have done if you'd been there. Then look at the product your students produce. Again, in the worst case, you'll just have to reteach it, but if you've chosen the right sub, the lesson is completed on time, and you stay on track for a successful school year.

Oddly, the quality of my day is dictated more by who I'm subbing for than by the subject I'll teach, or the students I'll teach it to. If "my teacher" leaves lesson plans and high expectations, the day is usually productive and upbeat. But, if my teacher leaves busy work and the expectation that nothing will be accomplished while a sub is there, then the students are bored, nothing is learned, and a day of school is wasted.

Talk to the students. They know who cares about the job and who's just killing a day. They'll tell you if the sub spent all day reading the newspaper or sending text messages. They'll tell you if the sub engaged the class, tried to teach, or took the time to learn some of the student's names.

Used effectively, substitutes can become another tool in a successful teacher's toolbox. I know that I'm the most effective when the host teacher makes me a part of his or her team.

Children are intuitive, and they feed off their teacher's attitude. When the teacher makes the sub an important, integral part of the team, the students treat the sub accordingly. Likewise, if the teacher treats the sub as unprofessional or somehow less than competent, so do the students.

Cultivate relationships with several subs. Have several subs to turn to when you need to take a day off. This is especially helpful when you have to do so with no notice. Illness and family emergencies are not times to have to worry about your lesson plans. Take the time off with the confidence that your students are in the hands of someone you trust.

Your students will develop and nurture relationships with substitutes at the same time you do. In fact, their impressions will help you in forming your own impressions. Remember, what's good for them is good for you (and vice versa)!

It's never easy for teachers to leave their class with someone else, but occasionally you're going to have to do it. Your students' success or failure on those days will be largely determined by how well you prepare now, before your absence, and by how well you prepare your students to accept the substitute teacher. Get ready now: your students are depending on you!

MUST-KNOW INFO

Strategies for Helping
Hyperactive Students

*Liana Heitin, MA Ed,
Cross-Categorical Special Education*

As a resource teacher in Phoenix, I had a brilliant and hyperactive student named Rudolpho. During my first year with Rudolpho, he was placed in a loud, active, general education third-grade classroom in which his teacher praised creativity and encouraged students to learn from one another. Rudolpho thrived that year, gaining nearly three grade levels in reading fluency and finding his place as a leader among his peers. The next year I saw a sharp increase in Rudolpho's energy level and a decline in his behavior. In our small reading groups, within five minutes of direct instruction he was shouting out or prodding the student next to him. He was often caught running in the hallways and roughhousing in PE. A few weeks into the school year, he had made little academic progress and his antics were worsening. When I spoke with his general education teacher, Ms. Mallon, a young, authoritarian teacher known for keeping an orderly classroom, she looked surprised. "He's never been a behavior problem in my class," she said. "He's quiet and finishes his work."

I invited Rudolpho's mother in for a chat. Looking worn when she came in, she confessed that she was losing patience with her son. He blew into the house everyday after school like a tornado. She'd bought him a trampoline but even an hour of jumping did not calm him. She said Rudolpho had admitted that he sometimes asked permission to leave Ms. Mallon's class and go to the bathroom, where he would lock himself in a stall and jump up and down as fast as possible. Then he would crumple up a ball of toilet paper, hold it over his mouth, and scream into it. The imagery was comical but the implications were heart-wrenching "He said he feels a heavy weight on his shoulders when he's in her class," his mom explained. It pained me to realize that school was not just distressing Rudolpho—it was causing him physical suffering. His rowdiness took a toll on us, but restraining his energy took a much larger toll on him.

This precocious nine-year-old had tried to develop a coping mechanism, but his parents and I were paying the price for each moment he bottled his energy to sit quietly in class. Many hyperactive students are not as self-aware as Rudolpho and counter a period of stifled energy with more negative releases—by punching another student at recess or tossing paint in art class. Although all students need to unwind when class is dismissed, students with hyperactivity feel a magnified sense of release and act out in more pronounced ways. For them, unstructured environments such as hallways and bus rides can become perilous, tempting places.

Having worked with a hundred children like Rudolpho, I've found it helps to think of a student's energy as water flowing through a hose. If you put a kink in the hose, the water backs up and pressure builds. When the kink is released, a torrent of water flows out or the hose may even flail about wildly. Likewise, asking students with ADHD or other hyperactivity disorders to sit still for long periods of time causes them escalating tension. Their energy cannot be diffused or diverted: it must be released.

Just as it is best to keep the hose untangled and let the water flow steadily, it is best to give hyperactive students some opportunities to unleash their energy throughout the day—not only during PE and recess. Rudolpho should not have to bear the "heavy weight" on his shoulders and his parents should not pay the consequences for a sedentary school day.

How can teachers give students optimal time to release energy? Here are a few ways to keep these students active without disrupting class. These tips apply mostly to elementary students, but can be modified for middle or high school students as needed.

- Give the student a classroom job that requires getting up and moving around—e.g., materials manager, paper collector, or message deliverer.
- Assign the student two desks that are across the room from each other. Between lessons or activities, allow the student to switch desks.
- Use masking tape to mark off a square on the floor around

the student's desk. Designate this as the student's area. He
can work anywhere within this space (on the floor, standing up, or at the desk).

- Make the student a helper or tutor whenever possible.
  This will allow for movement about the room and will
  encourage leadership rather than class-clown behavior.
- Devise a tacit signal with the hyperactive student. If the
  student needs a break, she can flash the signal (perhaps a
  thumbs up or the O.K. sign) and leave the room or go to
  a designated area for two minutes.
- Put the tissue box as far away from the student's desk as
  possible. Give the student permission to get tissues as
  needed.
- Replace the student's chair with an inflatable cushion or
  large exercise ball (some of which have three short legs
  for balance). This will encourage the student to activate
  the core muscles, which can be tiring, and to sit upright.
- Give the student a means of acceptable fidgeting, such as
  a Koosh ball or keychain to play with. (Enforce strict rules
  regarding the toys—confiscate them if they hit the floor,
  become a distraction, or are passed to another student.)

Be sure to monitor when these outlets are used. If two-
minute breaks are necessary during the math warm-up each
day, the issue may be avoidance rather than a need to release
energy.

Rudolpho, like most fourth graders, coveted his teacher's

approval, yet earning it came at a physical cost to him and an emotional cost to his parents, other teachers, and his peers. Many students cannot save their outbursts for the bathroom like Rudolpho and are labeled behavior problems. In this child's case, we found ways to help him before he internalized feelings of inadequacy. Students with hyperactivity need frequent outlets, but they also need teachers who understand their silent struggle and find creative ways to help them reach their potential.

MUST-KNOW INFO

Teaching the Gifted and Talented

Amy Figueroa, NBCT EC Gen, First-Grade Teacher

Working with children who have been identified as gifted and talented is a unique challenge for any teacher. As an ESE-certified (exceptional student education) teacher who has worked with these children for ten years, I have learned many tricks that can be adapted to any classroom. Whether that class is filled with ESE students, or with one gifted student who stands out, keeping the gifted and talented child engaged and learning gives any teacher an opportunity to be creative and can be a very rewarding experience. Here are some of the "tricks of the trade" I've picked up in my own training and through on-the-job experience:

1. There are many different ways for a child to learn and to interact with fellow students, but it gets tricky when several of these children are used to being "the best." When a learner is used to being the best, putting him into a group of "the bests" creates an extremely competitive

situation, often to the detriment of each child. One way to teach students to work together is through cooperative learning groups. It does take time and patience, but in the end it is rewarding and much more productive. There are many ways to group students for maximum educational benefit; some examples:

- Ability grouping—have all the students with the same ability level work together in one group.
- Random grouping—group students according to arbitrary categories, such as those whose birthdays are in the month of October, or everyone who is wearing a red shirt today.
- Multi-intelligence grouping—some children are strong in language skills, others in numbers manipulation. This grouping places one child with a strength in each intelligence type in the group so they can work together to problem solve using individual strengths for the good of the group.

2. When having children work together in a group environment, have each member be responsible for a job within the group. These jobs are almost limitless, but some of the most common include:

- recorder
- researcher
- organizer
- presenter

and so on, using strengths from each intelligence type.

Make sure you have an idea of the expected outcome. The use of rubrics makes this much easier to organize and set guidelines. A great website to access for further information is www.rubistar.com.

3. Student-generated tests—using key words or concepts, have the students compile questions that will assess the skills taught. Two great websites for help with this are www.quia.com and www.quizlet.com. In orchestrating these tests, you can set guidelines for your students, such as a combination of types of questions. For example, you might guide them to construct a test consisting of five true/false, three fill-in-the-blank, and two open-ended questions. You can edit each (at least for comprehension and clarity), and redistribute them to the students at random.

4. Backward assessment—one way to approach this concept is to provide the answers in a word bank. Guide students to create the questions based on the lesson's content and prescribed education standards. The students will generate a critical-thinking question based on the answer that you provide. This takes a lot of modeling. Prior to this assignment, it is imperative that you review examples of both poor and good examples of tests, in order to give students a clear understanding of your expectations.

5. Make, swap, and solve—as a mid-concept assessment, have the children practice the skill by making their own questions or problems. This practice works best with math, but can be successful with other subjects with care-

ful attention and preparation. Set clear boundaries for the students: for example, you might say "no numbers higher than ___." Once the students have created their tests, collect and randomly pass them out to their classmates. The recipients must solve the problems, which allows you to assess their comprehension twice—once by reviewing the created test, and a second time by correcting the answers given by the test taker.

MUST-KNOW INFO

Creativity and flexibility are the cornerstones of the learning philosophies described here. To successfully engage and challenge these exceptional children, it is important to cull their strengths and assist them in the acquisition of an ability to work within a cooperative environment while building on their individual strengths. Even at a very young age, these gifted and talented children have an amazing capacity to "think outside the box." As a professional educator, your creative skills will be continually tested—and sometimes stymied—while being part of the exciting process of helping to guide and challenge these special students.

I n nearly every K-12 school in our nation, some system is in place for scheduled conferences between teachers and parents of the students they teach. It is increasingly common to have students take an active role in these conferences also. Whether one teaches at the elementary, middle, or high school level, it is important to make the most of these valuable opportunities to improve student performance, strengthening the relationship between teachers, students, and parents, and increasing the likelihood of support at home for what is occurring in the classroom.

Students learn best when parents are actively involved in their children's schools. Great teachers seize opportunities for parent involvement, recognizing that when parents and teachers work together, students achieve at higher levels, demonstrate more positive behaviors and attitudes, and take a more active role in their own education. The key to successful conferences lies in effective communication and careful planning and involves the teacher, the parent(s), and the student.

Teacher Roles

For teachers, conferences are an opportunity to optimize the role of the parent in supporting the learning that is occurring in the classroom. To ensure success, teachers should carefully plan for every aspect of the conference, including the following:

- Create a realistic schedule for each conference and adhere to it. Post this schedule outside the classroom door if more than one conference is scheduled.

- If the possibility exists that parents will wait outside the classroom for their conference to begin, provide comfortable chairs, coffee or water, and reading material about your classroom or school.

- Prior to the conference, have parents complete a preconference survey to identify their interests, concerns, and expectations.

- Arrange the conference area within the classroom with adult-sized chairs and table.

- Remember that parents are people, too. Make them feel comfortable. Smile often and speak in a positive tone even when being direct and honest about areas of concern.

- Be prepared for parents who are non-English speaking.

- Prepare a discussion agenda for the conference.

- Try to listen as much as you speak. No one knows their child better than the child's parent(s). Endeavor to work as a team with the parent(s) to support the child.

- During the conference, be prepared with personalized notes and comments about the student. Provide written expectations for student work and behavior as well as examples of student work, including quizzes, tests, homework, and class work.
- Provide suggestions for home activities that will support the educational program.
- End the conference on a positive note and with a plan for future success.

Parent Roles

For parents, conferences are an opportunity to find out how their child is performing academically as well as socially and emotionally. They may want to find specific ways they can support their child at home to build on strengths and overcome challenges. Expect parents to arrive prepared to ask questions. You may even want to provide a list of appropriate questions for parents to ask, such as:

- What skills will my child learn in this grade or subject area this year?
- How are you teaching state or district standards and assessing whether my child is learning them?
- What are your expectations for homework? Has my child completed all homework assignments this year?
- How are my child's work habits? Does he or she use time wisely at school?

- Does my child read at the level you would expect for a student in this grade?
- Does my child qualify for any special academic programs?
- Does my child get along well with other students in the class?
- What can I do at home to help my child be more successful at school?

Student Roles

In recent years, many schools have moved from traditional parent-teacher conferences to student-led conferences in which the teacher plays a much less active role while the student takes the lead role in communicating with his or her parents what has been learned and to what extent. However, even if the conference is more traditional in structure, it is important to consider the student's perspective in his or her performance at school. Consider the following ideas for student-led conferences or simply for student participation in the conference process:

- Have students invite their parents to the conference, letting them know specifics about what will occur.
- Have students share their educational goals.
- Have students prepare examples of their best work.
- Have students analyze their strengths and weaknesses.
- Have students create and maintain a portfolio of their work throughout the year that can be shared at conferences.
- Have students write reflections on their grades and work habits.

- Have students rate the subjects and skills they like best and explain why.
- Have students complete a form rating themselves on a variety of skills and habits.

Conferences can be an extremely valuable opportunity for teachers, parents, and students to positively impact the student's education. Quite honestly, conferences can also be a waste of time for the teacher, parent(s), and student. By following the above guidelines, teachers can minimize the chances of the latter and maximize the likelihood of the former. The more actively teachers plan for success at conference time, the more likely it is that students will learn and that parents will support their child's teachers.

Students will view their teacher as either a friend or a foe. You are either fighting on the same side or you are the enemy in a war with rules that only the student knows. It is important as a teacher to gain students' trust, as this is the quickest way to win the war and focus on academics, but there is a fine line to walk. I have developed some ideas on maintaining a professional balance between being a friend and a teacher.

Behavior Management—In any classroom it is important to have and clearly express your expectations for students' behaviors. Close your eyes and picture what a perfect classroom looks like, and then teach those expectations and behaviors. The behaviors that students choose to exhibit are going to make your classroom either a pleasure or a war zone. In order for them to make correct behavior choices, students need to be taught what those correct choices are. Once the choices are taught, they need to be retaught. And once they are retaught, there will always be a few students who will need a refresher, so teach the correct choices again. After a long weekend or spring break, those correct behaviors may need to be reviewed again. I spend about three weeks on behavior and expectation training at the beginning of each school year, and I find that once the students have adopted these behaviors, the balance of the school year can be used for real academic progress.

Consistency—One of the first ways to gain a students' trust is by being consistent. Consistency in everything that happens within the classroom on a daily basis will help the students feel safe with you. Students will learn to expect how you are going to react and what the consequences and rewards will be. If students come into a classroom where the rules change every day or every week they will rebel and begin phase one of the student war on authority. On the other hand, if your rules are the same everyday and the students feel certain that those rules will not be changed on a whim, they will learn to comply and academic learning can begin.

Trust—The population of students that I work with is emotionally handicapped due to abuse and neglect at some point in their childhood. I have to gain their trust early in the school year in order for them to succeed in their educational goals. These students are all looking for someone to believe in them; someone to think that they can succeed in achieving their goals. Many of them have been told they can't do it, they are stupid, and they will never amount to anything. Is it any wonder that they believe they are failures? An enormous part of gaining their trust is showing them that the classroom is a safe place to try, even if they don't know how to do something. In order to gain their trust I must show them that no one is going to laugh at them if they get a question wrong or they don't know how to pronounce a word. I teach them that the smallest success is still a success. For every child, but especially the students of this population, real trust begins when they use their failure as a spring board for success.

Meeting Their Needs—This is the foundation for most of what I do in my classroom. I must meet the needs of the students in order for them to be ready to learn. If they are hungry, they will not be able to learn, so I have chips and cereal at the ready. If they need to vent or cry or shout, they are not ready to learn, so I have a quiet area in the back of the room. If they just need to talk, I have a desk next to mine that is always available. Meeting each student's individual needs is the key to guiding that student toward the next step of learning.

The war is never really won, but using some of these basic classroom techniques will give you a step up, and you might just become a teacher the students will always remember— the teacher they will recall as having been "a good friend."

MUST-KNOW INFO

Planning for Effective Classroom Management

Michael Lubelfeld, Ed.D., Assistant Superintendent and Educational Leadership Specialist

One of the greatest challenges teachers face is classroom management. Some call it discipline, others organization. Whatever the title, in my experiences, I have observed that effective classroom management and organization can turn a teacher's classroom into a learning laboratory for students of all ages. While there is much written about methods of management or discipline, I firmly believe that effective planning and delivery of instruction yield the most effective and engaged classrooms for students. Ingredients for effective classroom management include:

- dignified treatment of students at all times
- living belief that all students can learn
- realization that the learning environment is special and enriching
- a commitment that students' voices should be heard

loudly and clearly in an effort to create and sustain the most socially just classrooms

- believing every day and every lesson should be experiences of success

A lesson/unit design tied to effective organization and classroom management creates a learner-centered environment. When students are engaged in the learning experiences, their behavior is at or above behavior expectations in the classroom. Meaningful learning experiences can be selected for their usefulness in attaining the objectives. Relating the objectives to the learning tasks and tying them to the evaluation measures promote learning and exploration in a well-organized, safe, and orderly learning environment.

An example of how effective instruction leads to meaningful management is presented here through U.S. history, but the subject is used merely as an example; any subject matter or content can be substituted. The main points for the reader to gain and apply are related to the three "Es": *effectiveness* of instruction, *engagement* of students, and *commitment* to excellence.

As a result of this sample instructional unit in middle school U.S. history, students will be able to apply their knowledge of a specific time period in U.S. history (1870–1900) by gathering, processing, and presenting data. Learning experiences can be organized by assigning areas of concentration such as civil rights or women-in-history, as well as by time periods such as Civil War and Reconstruction, 1870–1900). The learning experiences can be evaluated with rubrics, product guides, and other measures. Content for this unit builds upon the chronological fifth or eighth grade scope and sequence of U.S. history from 1787 to present day.

Sample behavioral objectives for this unit might include the following:

- Students will know that history can be organized/divided into five areas: civil rights, women in history, science and technology, politics, and war and conflict.
- Students will learn how to gather data by doing research.
- Students will learn how to process/think about information they acquire.
- Students will apply the knowledge they gain to a presentation for their classmates or teacher by selecting from multiple types of product ideas on their chosen history area from the time period. Students will demonstrate knowledge by presenting key concepts and ideas with their presentation.
- Students will apply thinking skills by analyzing their topics' historical implications.
- Students will apply their communication skills by giving a well-focused and well-organized presentation.

Another key element of effective classroom management is the articulation of expectations at the start and end of student projects. Teachers are encouraged to use product guides and rubrics to assess student work. Students thrive in a structured and orderly environment and flourish when they know what is expected of them; there are no surprises for them in behavior or in learning. A rubric or product guide that identifies key concepts can be used for assessment. Teachers can measure the degree to which students know and understand the factual and analytical material. They can measure students' thinking or reasoning abilities, and they can also measure the quality of student communication—written, oral, and expressive—which integrates with writing assessment as well.

Essentially, following the lessons contained in the three Es (*effective* instruction, *engagement* of students, and commitment to *excellence*) will lead any teacher to a well-managed classroom with a minimum of behavioral interruptions. Classroom management can be a source of happiness and joy instead of anxiety and frustration. Focusing on the integration of lesson design, student engagement, and clear assessment will guide all teachers, new and veteran, to an ideal environment suitable for learners of all ages to succeed.

The Writers

Christa Allan is a writer and teacher in Louisiana where she lives with her husband, Ken, and their three cats. She's also mom to Michael, Erin, Shannon, Sarah, and John; mom-in-law to Andrae, and grammy to Bailey, Emma, and Hannah. Visit Christa at www.christaallan.com.

When **Donna Amato** isn't writing she works as a nurse. She lives with her four children and the family cat. She has published several stories in online magazines and print anthologies. Donna is currently working on her first novel.

Chris Bancells is a writer and teacher who lives in Bel Air, Maryland, with his wife (his inspiration) and his dog (his comic relief). His writings on books, life in and around Baltimore and wherever the two might meet, can be found online at http://runningbowline.com.

Diane Gonzales Bertrand is writer-in-residence at St. Mary's University in San Antonio, Texas. She writes fiction for family reading, loves to read and write poetry, and enjoys writing memoirs.

Pam Bostwick's many articles have appeared in magazines, newspapers, and anthologies, including several Chicken Soup for the Soul books. Although she is legally blind and hearing impaired, she enjoys a fulfilled life. She loves her country home, the beach, playing guitar, and is a volunteer counselor. She has seven children and ten grandchildren. She happily remarried July 7, 2007. E-mail her at pamloves7@verizon.net.

Ellie Braun-Haley designs programs for both adults and children. She presents workshops in creative movement and creative dance for kindergarten teachers and she enjoys her hobby, writing. Visit evrcanada.com and look for some of Ellie Braun-Haley's books.

Mickey Burriss has written for *The State* newspaper, *Anderson Independent Mail* newspaper, *Living in South Carolina*, the magazine for electric cooperatives, and fiction for *The First Line* and *Blue Cubicle Press*. As a member of the South Carolina

Writers Workshop, Mickey participates in their critique group and workshops. He also attends the Sandhill's Writers Conference in Augusta, Georgia.

Elynne Chaplik-Aleskow, Founding general manager of WYCC-TV/PBS and Distinguished Professor Emeritus of Wright College in Chicago, is an author, public speaker, and award-winning educator and broadcaster. Her nonfiction stories and essays have been published in magazines and newspapers and are anthologized in *Chicken Soup for the Chocolate Lover's Soul, The Wisdom of Old Souls, Forever Friends,* and *My Father Is My Hero* (2009). Visit her website at http://lookaroundme.blogspot.com.

Mary Cook is a UK-based freelance writer and former newspaper reporter whose articles, poems, and short stories have appeared in numerous publications, both in print and online. Her latest e-book, *Collywobblers: Perverse Verse for Guys and Ghouls,* can be found at: http://inkspotter.com/publications/books/collywobblers.htm.

Terri Elders, LCSW, a lifelong freelance writer, is a public member of the Washington State Medical Commission. She lives with husband, Ken Wilson, two dogs, and three cats in the country near Colville, Washington. Write her at telders@hotmail.com.

Nancy Engler lives in Arizona with her husband, two daughters, and two dogs. She enjoys writing children's literature. Her stories and poems have been published in a variety of places including *Wee Ones, Boy's Quest,* and *Our Little Friend.* In her spare time Nancy loves to read, paint, and draw.

Scott Gill is a husband, a father of four, and a writer. He teaches junior-high English and coaches basketball at the J. W. Williams Middle School in Rockwall, Texas. You can e-mail him at st_gill@charter.net.

Cynthia Hamond is in more than thirty-five publications including books in the Chicken Soup for the Soul series, *Stories for the Heart, Woman's World* magazine, American Greetings cards, and bible study aides, and is a King Features Syndication recurring author. She received two awards and was featured in *Anthology Today.* Two stories have been made for television. Visit her at CynthiaHamond.com

Donna Hedger originally comes from New York, but has lived in Florida most of her life. She is the wife of a wonderful husband, and the mother of three awesome teenage boys. Donna enjoys photography, gardening, writing, church activities, and learning new things.

Miriam Hill is coauthor of *Fabulous Florida* and a frequent contributor to Chicken Soup for the Soul books. She's been published in *The Christian Science Monitor, Grit, St. Petersburg Times, Sacramento Bee* and *Poynter Online.* Miriam's manuscript received Honorable Mention for Inspirational Writing in a *Writer's Digest* writing competition.

Louis A. Hill, Jr. authored three books and many articles. He earned a Ph.D. in structural engineering, designed bridges and buildings, and joined the engineering faculty at Arizona State University. He retired an Emeritus Dean of Engineering from the University of Akron. He is listed in *Who's Who in America*.

Colleen Ferris Holz is a freelance writer who lives in Appleton, Wisconsin, with her husband and two sons. She is also a volunteer coordinator for a mentoring program for families living in poverty. She is currently researching effective mentoring methods to write a guidebook for volunteers.

Abha Iyengar is a writer, poet, cyberartist, scriptwriter, and photography enthusiast. She has recently produced a poem film titled 'Parwaaz"(flight). Her work has appeared in Chicken Soup for the Soul books, *Knit Lit Too, The Simple Touch of Fate, Arabesques Review, Kritya, riverbabble, Flashquake, Citizen 32*, and others. Visit her website, www.abhaiyengar.com. Contact her at abhaiyengar@gmail.com.

Becky Kelley is a mother, wife, college instructor, and free-lance writer, not always in that order. Becky has been writing on and off since she won a local writing contest in 2003.

Mimi Greenwood Knight is a freelance writer living in South Louisiana with her husband, David, children Haley, Molly, Hewson, and Jonah, and a delightful menagerie of pets. Her work has appeared in *Parents, Working Mother, American Baby, Living Magazine, Today's Christian Woman, In Touch, HomeLife, At-Home Mother, Christian Parenting Today, Sesame Street Parents*, and a spattering of anthologies.

Nancy Julien Kopp draws on her Chicago childhood and many more years of living in the Flint Hills of Kansas for her inspirational nonfiction and memoir stories. Many of her family memories are published in anthologies, including, Chicken Soup for the Soul series and *Guideposts*, as well as in magazines, newspapers, and e-zines. Contact her at kopp@networksplus.net.

Kathryn Lay is a full-time writer in Texas, the author of over 1,500 magazine and anthology pieces as well as four children's books and a book for writers. You can learn more about her writing, teaching, and speaking at www.kathrynlay.com.

John J. Lesjack, a retired educator, has been published in several Chicken Soup for the Soul books, the *San Francisco Chronicle Sunday Magazine, Grit*, and other national publications. He maintains contact with several of his former students but has changed their names in his stories. Contact him at Jlesjack@gmail.com.

Delores Liesner has been published in anthologies,magazines, and on the Internet. She is a survivor of PMS and still loved by Ken. Delores' eight grandchildren have dubbed her "Hyper-grandma". She credits her Native-American heritage for foundations of faith, storytelling humor, and herbal lore. Her writing goal is to "publish" the hope she has received through the "Waymaker," Jesus. She welcomes contact at ds1917mail@yahoo.com.

Michelle Mach lives in Colorado. Her stories have appeared in several anthologies, including *Classic Christmas* and *Chicken Soup for the Coffee Lovers Soul*. Learn more about Michelle at www.michellemach.com.

Rosemary McKinley has had an essay published online by the Visiting Nurse Association. Another essay for Dreyfus Funds landed her a profile in the November 2006 issues of *Money* and *Fortune* magazines. Rosemary has had three poems published in *Lucidity* over the last few years. Another one was recently published in *LI Sounds*. In April, an article written by the author on an historical home was published in the *Peconic Bay Shopper*. You can email Rosemary at noonon30@optonline.net.

Linda Mehus-Barber lives with her loving husband, affectionately known as "The Buffalo," and their two dogs and cat, in the seaside community of Crescent Beach. She currently teaches at Regent Christian Academy in Surrey, British Columbia.

Theatre professional **Susan Merson** has had her fiction published in *Democrat's Soul* (HCI Books), *Nice Jewish Girls* (Penguin Plume), and *Lilith Magazine*, among others. Her first novel, *Dreaming In Daylight*, workshopped at Bread Loaf in '07, will be out from blocpress in February '09. *Your Name Here*, her book on solo performance, is available at Amazon.com. Visit her at www.susanmerson.com.

Val Muller currently teaches high school English and writes in her spare time. You may contact her at mercuryval@yahoo.com.

Todd Outcalt is the author of seventeen books, including the HCI titles *The Best Things in Life Are Free* and *The Healing Touch*. He lives in Brownsburg, Indiana, with his wife and two children.

Diane Payne teaches creative writing at the University of Arkansas-Monticello. She is the author of two novels, *Burning Tulips* and *A New Kind of Music*. She has been published in hundreds of literary magazines and numerous Chicken Soup for the Soul books. More info can be found at: http://home.earthlink.net/~dianepayne/.

Carrie Pepper is a Sacramento, California, freelance writer who has written on a variety of topics, including health/sports, the environment, and natural resources, for local and national publications. She is currently working on a collection of short stories and a memoir about her brother who was killed in action at Khe Sanh, Vietnam, and whose body was never recovered. Carrie is also a member of the American Society of Journalists and Authors (ASJA), the nation's leading organization of independent non-fiction writers. You can read more about her at www.carriepepper.com.

Linda Kaullen Perkins's short stories, articles, and essays have appeared in various publications, including *Chicken Soup for the Chocolate Lover's Soul*, *Chicken Soup for the Soul Kids in the Kitchen*, *Country Woman* magazine and *Woman's World* magazine. Visit Linda at www.lindakperkins.com.

Elizabeth Phillips-Hershey, Ph.D. has coauthored a middle-grade children's book, *Mind Over Basketball: Coach Yourself to Handle Stress*, (November 2007, Magination Press), and has numerous children's nonfiction stories published in *Appleseeds* and *Faces* (Cobblestone Press) and the Chicken Soup for the Soul series. Recent adult publications include "The Aeolian Islands" (2005) and "Sailing the Lycian Coast" (2008) in *Latitudes and Attitudes*, a sailing journal.

Charmi Schroeder has contributed to *Chicken Soup for the Dieter's Soul* and *Chicken Soup for the Recovering Soul: Daily Inspirations*. She is currently submitting her first novel to agents and publishers. She has appeared on several national television shows and in "Sweatin' to the Oldies 3." She is working on a lighthearted memoir about her adventures in weight loss. She can be contacted at SCCharmi@aol.com.

Michael Jordan Segal, M.S.W., married his high school sweetheart, Sharon, and became a father to their daughter, Shawn. Mike is a social worker at Memorial Hermann Hospital in Houston, Texas, and is currently working on two book projects: an autobiography and an anthology of his short stories. Mike's CD of twelve of his inspiring stories, *Possible*, is available on his website. He is also a popular inspirational speaker, sharing his recipe for success, happiness, and recovery. Please visit his website, www.InspirationByMike.com, or call Sterling International Speakers Bureau, toll-free in the USA/Canada, at 1-877-226-1003 for more information.

Joyce Stark lives in northeast Scotland and recently retired from local government. She has written a travel guide to the U.S.A., based on her travels throughout the States. She has also written a children's series aiming to teach a second language to very young children. Contact her at joric.stark@virgin.net.

Diane Stark is a teacher, a writer, a wife, and a mother. She writes about the things that are most important to her, her family and her faith.

Susan Stephenson has been published in *Australian Traveller, Transitions Abroad*, and in several online zines. She blogs about children's literacy and literature at http://thebookchook.blogspot.com. You can find out more at Susan's website, www.susanstephenson.com.au.

Lois Greene Stone, writer and poet, has been syndicated worldwide. Poetry and personal essays have been published in several book anthologies. Collections of her personal items, photos, and memorabilia are in major museums, including twelve different divisions of the Smithsonian.

Jill Sunshine served as an English teacher for the Peace Corps in Malawi before returning home to San Diego to teach English and journalism at the same high school she attended. Her passions include reading, writing, and traveling the world with her husband, Aparajit. She may be reached at jillsunshine.writer@gmail.com.

Cristy Trandahl is a former teacher, tutor, and writer for the nation's leading student progress monitoring company. Today she works as a freelance writer while raising her children. Cristy's stories are published in dozens of nationally distributed books. Visit www.cristytrandahl.com for more.

Samantha Ducloux Waltz is an award-winning freelance writer in Portland, Oregon. Her personal essays can be enjoyed in books in the Ultimate series,

Chicken Soup for the Soul series, and A Cup of Comfort series, and a number of other anthologies. She has also published fiction and nonfiction under the names Samantha Ducloux and Samellyn Wood. Visit her at www.pathsofthought.com.

Donna Watson teaches first and second grade in El Cajon, California. She loves spending time with her family: husband, Gary, grown children, Denny, Jill, and Bree, "kids-in-law," Ana and A.J., and grandtwins, Ana Christina and Alexander Lee Watson. Donna enjoys camping, boating, and traveling with family and friends.

Woody Woodburn is a former award-winning sports columnist in Southern California who left the press boxes after being hit by a drunk driver in 2003. Now a freelance writer, Woody likes to run marathons and has the cleanest running shoes in town. He can be reached at Woodycolum@aol.com.

D. B. Zane is a writer and teacher. She has been published in Chicken Soup books and elsewhere. When not teaching or spending time with her three children, she coaches and judges middle school debate.

The Must-Know Experts

Lisa Bundrick has a New York State permanent certification as a school social worker for grades K-12 and is a Licensed Master Social Worker (LMSW). Her career-related experiences in the field of education include working with students and staff in charter and public schools as well as in a community college. As a school social worker, she works with students in individual, small group, and classroom settings, assisting them in developing skills and knowledge to enable their success in both academic and social settings. Her experience includes such areas as crisis intervention, developing functional behavior assessments and behavior intervention plans, academic advisement, career planning, and cover letter and resume writing. She is currently employed as an elementary school social worker in the state of New York.

Amy Figueroa has been an elementary school teacher in Broward County, Florida, for the past ten years. A graduate of Florida Atlantic University with a BA in Education, she also holds a National Board Certification as an Early Childhood/Generalist. Each year her class of gifted and high-achieving first-graders challenges her to find new and exciting ways to make learning a passion. She continues teaching where she began, at Silver Palms Elementary in Pembroke Pines, Florida.

D. C. Hall began his quest to be a public school teacher by becoming certified as a substitute teacher. He discovered (to his great surprise) that he enjoyed the flexibility and variety of substitute teaching, and decided to continue his teaching career as a full-time substitute while pursuing his master's degree. He looks forward to a future career as a community college professor. He lives in Broward County, Florida, with his pet, Helen.

Liana Heitin has taught students with special needs for the past five years as a public school teacher, reading specialist, and private tutor. She has a master's degree in cross-categorical special education and is trained in several research-based reading programs, including Lindamood-Bell Learning Processes. Currently, she works on the editorial staff at teachermagazine.org and writes for *Education Week* newspaper.

Michael Hornsby has been an educator for five years. After obtaining a bachelor's degree in art with a minor in English literature at Southern Illinois University, he spent many years going from one job to the next before deciding it was time to give something back to his community. He is now a reading and English teacher in a center for students with emotional and behavioral disorders in Broward County, Florida. Working every day with this unique population has given him a different perspective about managing impulsive behaviors.

Michael Lubelfeld, Ed.D., is the assistant superintendent for personnel services in North Shore School District 112 in Highland Park, Illinois. In addition, he is adjunct faculty member at National-Louis University in the Department of Educational Leadership. A public school educator for more than sixteen years, Lubelfeld has taught middle school students social studies, reading, and civics. Earning his doctorate in education in curriculum and instruction allowed Lubelfeld to test theories of learning in action.

Jennie Withers is a graduate of Boise State University and a fourteen-year veteran of teaching at the secondary level, with endorsement, in English, humanities, and coaching. She has taught language arts, reading, creative writing, and technical reading and writing during her career. The author of *Hey, Get a Job! A Teen Guide for Getting and Keeping a Job*, she also leads curriculum writing committees and has presented various lesson plans at education conferences.

Dr. Jeffrey Zoul is a principal with North Shore School District 112 in Highland Park, Illinois. He has worked as a teacher, coach, assistant principal, and principal at the elementary, middle, and high school levels in the State of Georgia, and served as adjunct professor of graduate studies at North Georgia College and State University. He has authored and coauthored four books, including *Improving Your School One Week at a Time*, *Cornerstones of Strong Schools*, and *The 4 CORE Factors for School Success*. Dr. Zoul has presented at national conferences on a wide variety of educational issues. He earned his doctoral degree from the University of Alabama and holds additional degrees from the University of Massachusetts at Amherst, Troy University, and the University of Southern Mississippi. He can be contacted at: jeffzoul@comcast.net.

About the Author

D r. Todd Whitaker has been fortunate to be able to blend his passion with his career. Recognized as a leading motivational speaker in the field of education, his message about the importance of teaching has resonated with hundreds of thousands of educators around the world. Todd is a professor of educational leadership at Indiana State University in Terre Haute, Indiana, and he has spent his life pursuing his love of education by researching and studying effective teachers and principals.

Prior to moving into higher education, he was a math teacher and basketball coach in Missouri and still holds a school record for most wins in a season at one of the high schools where he coached. Todd then served as a principal at the middle school, junior high, and high school levels. He was also a middle school coordinator in charge of staffing, curriculum, and technology for the opening of new middle schools.

One of the nation's leading authorities on staff motivation, teacher leadership, and principal effectiveness, Todd has written fifteen educational books including the national best seller, *What Great Teachers Do Differently: 14 Things That Matter Most.* Other titles include: *Teaching Matters, Great Quotes for Great Educators, What Great Principals Do Differently, Motivating & Inspiring Teachers,* and *Dealing With Difficult Parents (And With Parents in Difficult Situations).* Focusing on the areas of teacher leadership, instructional improvement, change, leadership effectiveness, technology, and middle-level practices, his books have sold over 750,000 copies.

Todd is married to Beth, also a former teacher and principal, who is a professor of elementary education at Indiana State University. They are the proud parents of three children; Katherine, Madeline, and Harrison.

Copyright Credits

(continued from page ii)